Veils of the Heart

A Sufi Woman's Spiritual Journey

Munirah Maclean

◆ FriesenPress

One Printers Way
Altona, MB R0G 0B0
Canada

www.friesenpress.com

Disclaimer:
This work describes actual events in the life of the author as truthfully as memory allows, to promote healing, clarity and connection. Dialogue has been adjusted for readability; composite characters are used and names have been changed to protect privacy. It is my sincere intention that no harm be caused to anyone in the telling, rather that it will facilitate truth and empower others to do the same in their own personal journey.

ISBN
978-1-03-832963-9 (Hardcover)
978-1-03-832962-2 (Paperback)
978-1-03-832964-6 (eBook)

1. BIOGRAPHY & AUTOBIOGRAPHY, WOMEN

Distributed to the trade by The Ingram Book Company

Veils of the Heart

Dedication

To all of those seeking truth with sincerity, may it find you.

Table of Contents

Acknowledgements

T he writing of this book really began with the publication of *Muslimah Who Fell to Earth: The Personal Stories by Canadian Muslim Women*, by Saima S Hussain (editor), and published by Mawenzi House, Toronto, in October 2016. https://www.mawenzihouse.com/

The good fortune of having a piece included in that anthology and meeting other Muslim women interested in writing at the Ottawa Book Fair inspired me to continue. My deep gratitude to all of you involved in that process.

We all have our stories, but other than *Medieval Mystics* and Thomas Merton's *The Seven Storey Mountain* (Merton, Thomas: The Seven Story Mountain, Harcourt, Brace, 1948), I did not know that spiritual memoir was a genre. Elizabeth Jarret Andrew and The Eye of the Heart Center (https://community. eyeoftheheartcenter.org/posts/62759111),

an online community focused on the mysterious, wondrous gift that writing is to us and to each other, transformed that into regular practice. The gift of this practice is its openness, its accessibility, and its inspiration. Friesen Press, a Canadian publishing service, has enabled me to present this book to you now. If it was in the hands of traditional publishers, constrained by commercial and ideological principles, it is unlikely that would ever have happened.

A vast source of joy and many adventures is my lifelong multi-dimensional collaboration with Dr. Joel Kreps (aka Dr. Ibrahim) and his Montreal family. This story is evidence of that, if any was ever needed. Our wonderful daughters,

Adilia, Amina, and Sara, are amazing women who have inspired and supported me throughout this process; their influence is nestled in every word. You have shown me that love is eternal.

My gratitude to Dr. Muhammad Isa Whaley, a friend on the path and an expert in so many aspects of Islamic Sufism. He gave his help with the glossary and suggested important refinements. His work on the translation and editing of many important texts of Tasawwuf is a gift to us all. See https://g.co/kgs/wdu2Q7h.

Professor 'Abd al-Haqq Godlas, PhD, managed to plow through the text and generously gave a professional eye through perceptive and insightful comments. He is a wonderful teacher and editor. As an authority with personal experience of contemporary Sufi orders, his insights are treasures.

David L. Sterling (aka Hajj Mustafa) showed me a great example of an independently published book of Sufi spiritual memoir. His 2022 book, *Journey in Grace, Gems Gathered from a Life on the Path* (ISBN 978-0-578-27444-7), is an inspiring example of a Sufi spiritual memoir. He is one of the people who creates a track up the mountain. By offering his wisdom on the process, he shared vital information and much-needed encouragement.

Thank you to all those who inspired and supported this book who are in this world and the next.

All Praise is to God and his servants.

Prologue

When I was sixteen, I had a dream. I walked through an intricately carved archway into an ancient city filled with colour and people. Stalls on either side of the street had tables of exotic goods, and voices called out in different dialects. It was a souk in the open air, of clear sky and sunlight. I did not know where I was, somewhere in the East, and I loved this place; it felt completely like home. The throng ahead of me parted, and facing me stood an old man, smiling. He wore a large turban and a dark green coat, reaching down to his calves. Above a long white beard, his blue eyes looked clearly at me, seeing me. He nodded acknowledgement. I nodded back. It seemed we had known each other for a while because he was my teacher.

"When the pupil is ready, the master appears." I do not know who said that, but I disagree. A jaded sixteen-year-old, I was more than ready. I was exhausted by the consequences of the disintegration of my family, the tragic death of my father, and my mother's breakdown. I lived in 70s London, UK, attending school, and doing my exams. For my art O-level, I did a gouache painting of the dream figure in a "faraway land." It was in the style of the Mughal paintings of court life I admired. The art department did not like it, and I got a C. That was a sign in two ways. First, I did not go on to study art, my best subject; second, this old man wasn't going to get me into university, my escape plan. So, I put aside the dream and moved on into literature and William Blake, classics and mythology, Eastern philosophy, and the Buddha.

Later, I studied religion and philosophy at the University of Lancaster. We studied texts, systems of thought, historical periods, anthropology, epistemology, and world religions. In our student-led societies, we invited speakers and teachers, some of whom came or sent representatives. The more desperate, or the less academically minded, lived in shared housing in the city of Lancaster, and we operated in what was then called the "Alternative Society." This was mostly made up of the kind of people who, in the 1960s and 1970s, were exploring alternative lifestyles. Some benefited from free student grants to study at universities, and some were able to manage on social welfare payments by living and eating collectively in run-down, low-rent housing. Through this network, we explored new spiritual ways and teachers, new workshops, and new dimensions. Although I had seen photos of many teachers with turbans on, I had yet to see any of the man from the dream. I told myself this was a "Jungian archetype," a dream image of my "inner wisdom," the Hierophant in the tarot deck, a symbol of a benevolent spiritual patriarch. However, experience taught me I couldn't rely on a patriarch; it was necessary to make my own way.

I went on to study education at the University of Durham, planning to leave England, go abroad to somewhere in Asia, and work teaching English as a second or foreign language. A British volunteer organization accepted me, but they didn't agree with that plan. They offered me a contract in northern Nigeria because that was where they needed teachers. Ironically, I had said in my interview that the only culture that I did not want to work in was a Muslim one because I knew it would be very difficult as a Western woman to do so. In desperation to escape Britain at that time, I accepted the contract anyway.

A month before I was to leave, I went on a spontaneous visit to the Swiss Alps for one last group event before my life changed irrevocably. I signed up for a weeklong workshop with a teacher called Michael Barnett, who I had met previously in Cambridge, UK, and in Berlin. He was the first teacher I had ever heard of who treated "spiritual energy"—otherwise known as "chi" or "prana"—as a substance that can be manipulated and shifted using movement, dance, mindfulness, and hands-on healing. I had been very impressed by his methods and was entranced by the person himself. He had a brilliant mind but a very flawed character, what is now known as a "dark triad personality" of narcissism, psychopathy, and scheming. His workshops were enormous fun, however, and filled with all kinds of interesting European people. The setting for this July event was a Hindu ashram in the Swiss Alps called Schwiebenalp,[1]https://sch-weibenalp.ch/gaestezimmer/?lang=en formerly a resort hotel and now a place for the disciples of an Eastern guru called Sri Babaji.

My life did change after that trip, but not in a way I could have imagined.

Sheikh Nazim at Schwiebenalp, 1984.

---

1 Schwiebenalp, Zentrum der Einheit (Centre of Unity), accessed November 7, 2024.

Why I Met My Sheikh

⁊ℓ

Around the campfire, the Western Swamis were dancing and chanting songs of praise to Krishna, doing a fire ceremony known as a "Yagnya." The doll statue had now been put to bed in an elaborate fashion, and the visiting guests from Michael's workshop had enjoyed a delicious vegetarian dinner served outside as we all sat around in a circle. Many of the participants in the workshop were past followers of "Bhagawan" Rajneesh (later Osho), as he was known at the time, and felt any inhibition on their part was a barrier to enlightenment. Subsequently, there had been tensions between naked lovers and celibate Hindus all week, and I didn't feel comfortable with either of these groups.

As I gazed into the flames, I wished I was more sociable. I didn't want to engage with most of the people there. I had been following the Christian faith for a couple of years and had tried to put some moral boundaries around my behaviour. Although I felt at that time personal ethical and moral guidelines were subjective, when confronted with behaviours that I instinctively felt were wrong or absurd, I found myself reacting. One of the few connections I had made was with an American Jungian analyst called Art. We had discussed many common interests, and I was relieved to find that he also considered himself a Christian. When he came up to me and told me that a Turkish Sufi Sheikh had just arrived on a visit, I was at once galvanized. A Sufi Sheikh? A real one, like a whirling dervish? I knew I had to meet this person, so as soon as I saw a distinguished-looking man wearing a turban and dressed in a white shirt, waist-coat, and sherwal (traditional Muslim-style wide trousers), I got up at once and went over to talk to him.

"Are you the Sufi sheikh?" I demanded before even introducing myself. There was no time to waste. I needed to meet this person and find out all there was to know about a real and authentic spiritual path. I was disenchanted with jumping around to loud music and psychodynamic circle time with the "energy group."

In answer to my question, he turned to face me, and there was an eternal pause as his warm brown eyes met mine. Whatever he was, he was handsome and comfortable in his masculinity in a way that the tortured liberal Christian men at my college in Durham were not. My interest burst into flame along with the bonfire, onto which one of the Swamis had just tipped a pot of sacred oil.

"Well, no," he confessed. "But I can take you to meet him if you like."

I didn't want to wait any longer.

One step, two steps, many steps . . . we walked up the smooth path through the meadow sprinkled with blue and yellow alpine flowers to the chalet where the Sufi Sheikh was staying. I was wrapped in a gold and crimson striped sheet, which covered the punk black T-shirt and drainpipe jeans I habitually wore at that time. The handsome Canadian, whose name was Ibrahim, was taking me to meet the Sheikh. He stopped and looked around. "Sheikh Nazim's staying in the chalet, but I don't see it," he said.

The sun was setting behind the mountain range, and it was quickly becoming dark. I have always had an intuitive sense of direction, and something was pulling me to follow the path going toward the right and down. I went in front. "Maybe it's this way," I suggested. Ibrahim followed, telling me about his recently com-pleted medical specialty in psychiatry and some of his Sufi experiences. Then we reached the perfect Swiss chalet, which had been hidden from below. In this crowded place, full of Western "spiritual seekers," it was curious and wonderful that nobody else was there. My impulsiveness had made me the first visitor.

A few weeks before, when I left the Christian college at the University of Durham where I studied, I had a strong conviction that the best religious path was rooted in worldly service, but I also had an aching unease about the course of my life. I wanted to do something to make things better for the world. Guided by my studies in philosophy and theology, I felt what was needed was an integra-tion of the spiritual disciplines of the East and the rigorous work ethic of the

West, the integration of the depth psychology of Jung and Greek pl
with the higher states of consciousness of Eastern mysticism. I was ver,
fortable with most of the social conditions and structures I had experienced.
The poverty and desperation I had seen in my travels had shocked me deeply,
and the cynicism, greed, and oppression of British society under Margaret
Thatcher repelled me.

As we made our way up a short pine staircase, our voices dropped to a whisper
as Ibrahim explained that Sheikh was an orthodox Muslim, so it was better to be
dressed in a way that covered the body and to understand that the cultural context
around him was very different from what I was used to. Ibrahim knocked on
the door, and after a few moments, we entered. Sheikh Nazim was sitting in this
room, alone. An older, small- statured man with a long grey and white beard, he
was wearing a large white turban wrapped around a green pointed hat. He wore a
long, dark green overcoat, and next to his chair was a walking cane. His face was
a combination of beauty and gentleness, with a smooth skin that glowed with an
inner light. In his right hand, he held what I recognized as "prayer beads." The
sparse room of the chalet was full; full of a light which bathed everything with a
gentle presence. I felt an almost palpable certainty that here was truth—"Haqq."
The simple wooden furniture just sang with it.

Whoever or whatever this person in front of me was, he had somehow
managed to combine a strong personal transcendence with a deep, joyful being
in the world. He didn't scowl like a Mullah or swing like a Rolling Stone. He was
just what he was, without superfluity or pretense. The truth is, I have never met
anyone like this. I was silenced and amazed.

As I stood just inside the doorway, wrapped in the crimson sheet, Ibrahim
introduced me. "As salaam alaikum, Sheikh. This is Jane."

"Djinn?!" joked Sheikh. I later learned this was a reference to an old Turkish
story about travellers being lured off their way by djinn in seductive female
forms. As neither of us laughed, not understanding the joke, he greeted me
more formally.

"Welcome," he said. "I am a Muslim."

A Muslim? The Muslims I had met in England were not like this. At the
university, they wore baseball caps and studied subjects like metallurgical
engineering. They were all male and went around in twosomes. Sometimes, a
group would get together to complain angrily about "capitalist ideology" or "the

colonialist political agenda." Most of the other students kept their distance. They were nasty rumours about them, also: they subjugated women, they cut people's hands off, and—the cruellest to my vegetarian sensibility—they slit the throats of lambs. It all made for a nasty, dark collage of black shrouds, machine guns, and gore. I had never connected this with the profound wisdom I had discovered in writings like the *Rubaiyat* of Omar Khayyam or the ghazals of Rumi, which I had studied as literature and poetry, not religious texts.

I sat on a low chair a distance away from him. "You have questions?" he asked. He clearly had the measure of me very quickly. I certainly had questions, a character trait which had often estranged teachers.

I launched into one of my most urgent theological problems. The dilemma between "destiny" and "free will": if this is a created universe run under divine decree, how can humans act autonomously? The standard explanation of this always seemed to trail off into "mind productions," to use a Buddhist term. I was intrigued to see how he would explain what I had interpreted as a kind of "passive fatalism" endemic to the declining traditions of the world of Islam— waiting for the whim of some distant deity to do to you whatever he happened to decide on a particular day. Behind it was the personal dilemma as to what I should do when circumstances were presenting me with an opportunity, such as my contract in Nigeria, which did not feel like the best thing for me to do.

This will be good! I thought. *How is he, a "determinist Muslim," going to explain this one?* "How do you know what the 'will of Allah' is?"

"Are you asking this because you are wanting to know truth, or because you are testing me?" was his reply.

I was surprised. Caught off guard. "Both," I answered.

He went into a short homily about the role of humanity, Adam in particular, and how they were the Caliphs of Creation by the will of God.

I was not receptive to his words because they did not align with my world view of a chaotic universe with divine intervention as something very ineffective against the "bad guys" oppressing and exploiting everyone else. I felt that he wasn't giving me "fresh, spontaneous answers," but instead he was restating a sacred text. When he had finished, I was still confused. I wondered what this had to do with whether I should go to Nigeria, what my personal destiny was. I was dreading the trip, which was now only five weeks away.

At that time, I was convinced that the only access to truth was through the inspired spontaneous utterance of highly evolved people, such as the Buddha. I did not have the concept of discovering truth by reflecting on the words of sacred texts, such as the Quran, to receive divine guidance.

I struggled to restate the question.

"I mean, how do you know what is the right thing to do? When you must decide a course of action, how do you know what is best?"

"Ah!" He looked at me directly, and I met his gaze. Now he had intuited my difficulty without me giving him any details. It was a theoretical question about what was a very practical issue.

I told him about the contract I had signed to go to Nigeria and teach.

He was shocked. "Why are you going there?" he demanded. "Where is your family?" He was appalled that I would even consider going to a strange, far-off country as a young single girl.

I explained I didn't have any family, or anyone who particularly wanted me around. I explained my mother was "ill," a euphemism for being too over-whelmed with her life to really care at that time. However, it was clear to him what I should be doing.

"Go back to London and take care of your mother," he ordered.

That was really the last thing I wanted to do, but I knew that cancelling the Nigeria contract was the right decision. Greatly relieved and reconnected with myself after months of my mind telling me the "right" thing to do, which was, in fact, the wrong thing, I felt certainty once again.

The next evening, everyone was told that the Sheikh would come down the hill from the chalet to address us in the assembly room of the hotel. Directly after Michael's group session, I went there and waited. The afternoon light left the room, and a few more people came in to sit and wait.

The small number surprised me, but I later understood that Michael was feeling threatened by the charismatic personality, who was getting a lot of atten-tion and interest, and so he had decided to give an impromptu talk and lead an "energy exercise" outside in the meadow. Michael saw everything as a competi-tion and needed to win by popular vote. The workshop guests had opted for the fun rather than the possible disapproval of what they perceived as a very conservative, traditional teacher. Sheikh did not hide his Islam or modify it in any way, and this was not acceptable to their mindset. From the point of view of Michael's group, religion was dead, God was dead, and the party continued.

As darkness fell, the head of the Ashram brought Sheikh, who walked slowly, holding his cane, and a hush fell on the room as we stared at this figure who was like a being from another world. His two travelling companions, my Canadian and a Cypriot American, also called Ibrahim, came in with him and sat on either side of the simple wooden chair that had been placed for him. Sheikh Nazim slowly looked around the room at the small audience and then closed his eyes and lifted his hands in duah. I didn't understand the words, but I felt a sudden seriousness and gravity in the occasion. I knew this was important.

The American Ibrahim asked for a glass of water for the Sheikh. Immediately, I got up. For some reason, I knew that it was very significant that I go and do this. I ran downstairs to the kitchen and searched frantically for a glass, finding a jam jar and filling it directly from the tap.

An older man I had never seen before came in and addressed me in a thick accent I didn't recognize. "Oh, English girl, calm down!" He found a plate and some biscuits and placed them on a tray with the jam jar. Smiling, he said, "Now you go. You have the honour of serving your Sheikh because you are now his servant."

Of course, I didn't fully realize the implications of what he was saying at that point.

Carefully and shaking a little, I put the tray down on the wooden floor in front of Sheikh Nazim. He nodded and lifted the glass and muttered some words in Arabic. He took three sips, then passed it to the American, who did the same, and then to Canadian Ibrahim. I had seen, for the first time, the breaking of a fast, and I had the amazing honour of giving the water and the biscuits. A Tradition tells us that "Allah rewards those who provide food and drink for people breaking their fast, and the reward can be the equivalent of their fast."

Then, the two Ibrahims rolled out some prayer mats they had been carrying, and with the Sheikh leading, they all performed the prayer of the sunset, Maghrib. Some of the audience left. Still fascinated, I stayed, but did not know what to do. After the prayer, Sheikh gave a small talk which, I felt, came from a stern place and was not like the jovial and amusing content I had heard previously.

His voice rose as he described the antics of Michael's group. "They are jumping and laughing. They do not realize they are jumping like fish in a net before they are dying. The Shaitan has them in his net."

Of the Hindu Babaji followers, he said, "Inshallah, they are sincere ones, and they are looking and serving as they have learned in their seeking, and we make duah for them for guidance."

On another occasion, in a morning talk, I remember him looking at the small group of us seated in front of him and saying, "Who is the best of you? Who is the most advanced in spiritual ways?"

He had caught our attention because, of course, everyone was hoping that he would acknowledge their own individual spiritual state. His eyes slowly scanned the room, which increased the dramatic effect. Then he turned and gestured toward a burly Hungarian man who had been brought across the border to work as the cook for the group, a task which involved spending all day and a lot of the night in the kitchen. "It is him! Because he is a humble one and because he is serving."

Everyone smiled but felt uncomfortable because up to that point, most people had ignored the tired, shy man who spoke little English. The cook wiped away his tears with his hands, still wearing his soiled apron.

This teaching of the value of service for spiritual development made a deep impression on me. It also resonated with the Christian values of service to society rather than leaving it and going off on retreat into a cave. It seemed that the "Sufi Way" was not just whirling in ecstasy like in Turkish tourist brochures for Konya visits but had profound implications for our material lives as well.

Someone asked the Sheikh about being a vegetarian, and his approach was interesting. He agreed that meat-eating, as it took place in the West, was excessive and unhealthy. He said that eating too much meat is "making hardness of heart." He recommended eating a "little meat," at least once every forty days (about one and a half months). He pointed to the canine teeth in his mouth as evidence that our bodies were designed to eat meat. Once again, he showed the flexibility and moderation, the acceptance of our material conditions and our spiritual responsibilities, at the heart of the path of Sufism. This approach was clearly defined and balanced; it seemed to hold the promise of spiritual understanding that we, the seekers, craved.

✤   ✤   ✤

I knew that in meeting Sheikh Nazim, I had discovered the genuine thing, the "real deal." He embodied an amazing presence in a room, and he had a light and sweetness that was a reflection of his sincere and devoted relationship with Allah. Here was a Sufi master who could take me to the levels of spiritual attainment I wanted. Having met the handsome Canadian Ibrahim, I also realized that it was possible for a Western person to follow an Eastern teacher and combine it with education, earlier knowledge, and personal insight. There were a couple of difficulties, however. The most personally significant seemed to be the Sheikh's insistence that his followers all be Muslim and then the expectation that I would assume a role that was completely alien—that of a traditional "Ottoman" woman, or the type of woman that he thought that should be. This would include wearing "hijab," dressing modestly, deferring to the males I was affiliated to, and perhaps marriage and raising children. My first response to this was largely negative, but I also knew that if I wanted to get to the vital teachings of the Sheikh, I would have to comply, eventually.

It was the start of my initiation into Sufism, an ancient tradition of wisdom that has unclear origins but, in the case of the Naqshbandi Order, is rooted in the original transmission of Prophet Muhammed (PBUH) and the first caliph and companion, Abu Bakr (*radiya 'llāhu 'anhu*). If my question had not been answered then, I do not know how my path would have continued. Sheikh Nazim was unique and extraordinary in that he was willing to engage in dialogue with a young and opinionated English girl, lost, looking for answers and in need of clear guidance.

Talking specifically about following the way of Allah and Sufism he had said to me before he left, "If it is in accordance with truth, justice, beauty, and love, then you know that this is the Way."

Later, I realized that the practice of Islam is the simplest, clearest expression of spiritual reality. I had tried many spiritual approaches—religions such as Buddhism and Christianity—and only in Islam did I feel complete. How do we know truth? Why can't we see it?

To follow the "will of Allah," we need to align ourselves with divine truth, which we recognize because it holds the principles of love, justice and beauty among other things. The correct response to the profundity of truth is submission and the only person who was able to explain that to me was someone who had experienced it himself.

I believe in destiny, but I also believe in free will. The two threads seem to twine together like the brightly coloured cord of a newborn baby. However you interpret it, something aligned to bring me the possibility of a radically different life from the one I had been living. I thought I had a choice, and in a way, I did, but—when I turned to my heart—I knew what I had to do.

Surat Al-'Anfal [verse 30] ... But they plan, and Allah plans. And Allah is the best of planners.

Ibrahim and Sheikh Nazim in the Alps, 1984

* * *

When I arrived back in London, I cancelled my flight and contract and faced the storm of "emergency" phone conversations and meetings called because of my last-minute decision not to go to Nigeria. I stayed with my mother in Mill Hill, and I started to look for a teaching job. I found a parental leave replacement vacancy in a school in the east end of London, where 95% of the students were Bangladeshi boys, the other 5% being working-class "East Enders" who resented the presence of these recent newcomers to the UK. The tension between the two groups had broken out into outright war with gang fights, stabbings, and protests. Eventually, the teaching staff went on strike, and that was the end of my brief teaching post.

As I was in London, I decided to take the opportunity to visit followers of Sheikh Nazim, whom Ibrahim had highly recommended. These were the people closest to the Sheikh when he was in England. I was nervous and excited as I carefully plotted my route across London using my A-Z map book.

Meryem

॰ஐ

After cancelling my teaching contract in Nigeria, I was adrift once more and trying to discern the new direction of my life. The latest "existential crisis," brought about by my first meeting with Sheikh, was now blooming. I clung to all the certainty I could sense. I knew I wanted to find out all I could about this centuries-old Sufi tradition and its leader. He was the most remarkable human being I had ever met, a combination of guru, personal guide, and an immersive experience in an ancient culture.

All I had been able to find in Islington Public Library was Idries Shah's *The Sufis*[2] and G. Gurdjieff's *Meetings with Remarkable Men*.[3]

Neither of these books told me very much or gave any significant details. There was nothing I could find that referred to this movement. There were the two Ibrahims, East Coast Jewish boys turned dervishes, and their extraordinary Sheikh, the turban-wearing people who drove into Schwiebenalp in a VW campervan on their way back to Turkish Cyprus. Their practice of orthodox Islam made them a complete anomaly in the "rebirthing" and "energy" scene of the time. Although "Canadian Ibrahim" had told me there were other Western converts to Islam, the people he referred me to were Turkish followers of the Sheikh who had been born Muslim. I reflected on this as I stubbed out my cigarette butt

---

2   Idries Shah, *The Sufis*, UK, Doubleday, 1964

3   G. Gurdjieff, *Meetings with Remarkable Men*, UK, Routledge, 1963.

on the upper floor of the double-decker bus taking me to Peckham, London as it turned onto Rye Street.

Ibrahim had given me a name and address to go and gather more information about the Sheikh. I felt a certainty that these must be the real Sufis, the Khwajagan Sufi masters referred to by Gurdjieff. I gripped the piece of torn paper with the details in my hand as I walked along the bustling High Street, looking at the numbers and names above the shops. The street consisted of low two- and three-storey houses with shops on the ground level. A wide variety of goods from many of the ethnic stores spilled out onto the pavement, "Proudly African," "Many Items 98p," and "Island Beauty Salon," I noticed on awnings and signs. Crowds of people from diverse backgrounds thronged the streets, wheeling shopping carts, and strolling in groups in "punk" regalia. Music blasted out of doorways and from "boom boxes" (portable stereos) carried on shoulders because of their size. It was easy to get lost in the multitude. I missed the shop and then had to count back, straining my neck to see above headscarves, neon hair crowns and hats.

At the address I had been given, I found a modest grocery shop with a green doorway and a large window crammed with products and flyers in Turkish and other languages. I stepped inside and smelled spices and meat. On the left were shelves packed to the ceiling with jars and cans of jams, vine leaves, and olive oil, and, higher up, brimless caps, prayer rugs, and shawls. On the right was a sizable, glass-covered, refrigerated counter with olives, yogourt, and plastic tubs of feta cheese in brine. At the far end, there was a butcher section with slices of dark meat and some containers with chopped-up chunks of animal. A thin lady with a flowered headscarf, apron, and slippers was loudly addressing in Turkish a tall, bearded man with a green knitted hat who stood behind the counter. He was nodding his head.

Unsure what to do, I waited near the doorway for the interaction to finish. It was over with a swish of the plastic ribbon curtain hanging at the back as the woman disappeared behind it.

The man, who I found out later was called Selim, saw me and moved along the counter until he was facing me from behind it. There was an awkward silence while I wondered which of my questions about the processes of Sufi initiation and enlightenment to start with. I sensed that perhaps that subject could wait, and I should try to figure out what was going on before that. "Is Hajja Meryem here?" I asked.

"Mery . . . EM!" he yelled and gestured toward the doorway that the lady had just gone through. I went through into a back room that was a combination kitchen, living room, and dining area. A worn red velour armchair was next to the doorway, and wooden chairs were lined up against glossy cream walls. A large chopping board was in the middle of a cluttered melamine table in the centre of the room, surrounded by fresh herbs and overripe vegetables—zucchini, eggplant, and tomatoes. A small white plate with a half-eaten jam sandwich was next to the chopping board. A plastic hamper of crumpled clothes was on top of a washing machine next to a sink full of dishes. In other areas, wooden crates were stacked with trays of apples, onions, and some large cardboard boxes with the printed logo, "Kingdom of Saudi Arabia." It was chaotic, and I felt comfortable right away. It was the last thing from "uptight."

The woman turned around from tending a huge pot on top of the gas stove. "Hello dearie," said Meryem, gesturing toward a chair. "What brings you here to see us?"

As I was sinking in the armchair, sipping from a glass of warm Turkish tea, Meryem quizzed me, establishing context and details with alarming speed.

"So, Dr Ibrahim sent you? Have you seen him?"

Once she had got sufficient information, she looked at me with shrewd consideration. "You want to know more about Islam?"

It's hard to admit, but I didn't want to know about external rituals and what rules I should follow. I was hungry for some mystical experience and gnostic wisdom, which I saw as something altogether separate. I thought I already knew everything I needed to about Islam because I had read a book or two about it as part of my required reading at Lancaster University. One of the monotheistic traditions for Arab people. Inaccessible and unrelatable otherwise. The Muslim buildings are lovely, but they don't have pictures.

As Meryem began her highlighted account of the Five Pillars, the observances of the faith of Islam, we were joined by her teenage daughter, who sat by the stove finishing her sandwich and nodding as her mother preached. Wearing faded jeans with a matching jacket, there was nothing that indicated that she was anything except a typical London teenager of that time. Neither of them seemed to be aware that they were representing an ancient lineage of Naqshbandi Khwaja masters, as described by Gurdjieff. The context was more like a Turkish version of *Coronation Street*.

"You want to get married?" Meryem startled me by asking suddenly, interrupting my distracted thoughts.

Now we were getting to the nugget of the matter as she saw it, after the tea and sweets. A young English woman had arrived who had met a handsome follower of Sheikh Nazim while on holiday. It was time to get serious because Muslims do not have casual relationships with the opposite gender. I really didn't know how to answer. Would they understand that I saw marriage as a pillar of the patriarchal system and the main vehicle for the subjugation of women? I had kept my copy of *The Second Sex*[4] with my pencilled notes in the margin throughout my travels, alongside the Bible. Again, I felt that this was not the right place for this conversation or that it was one I really wanted. I was wondering if perhaps they had a "Kwaja master" up in the attic that when they trusted me, I could access. I chose to say a non-committal "Well, maybe."

Ignoring my obvious lack of enthusiasm, Meryem generously plied me with advice, none of which I felt was relevant to my situation, how marriage is a partnership before Allah and how the gift of children is the "fulfillment of womanhood." The strangest thing to me was that I felt she really meant it.

Observing my puzzlement, she smiled and spoke. "You see, dear, it's like this. The man is the head, and the woman is the neck. The head turns in the direction that the neck points it." Smiling and crossing her arms, it became clear my interview was finished. Seconds later, I heard a pre-recorded call to prayer from somewhere farther away.

"Cat Stevens is a Muslim. His name is now Yusuf Islam," said the daughter kindly, to reassure me that I could still be hip and holy.

As I did not want to be caught up in prayer rituals at that time, after thanking them, I gathered my coat and bag.

In the shop, the head of the household was rinsing a plastic bowl from a hose pipe over a floor drain. I said goodbye, but he was so absorbed in the procedure he didn't seem to hear me.

My head was still full of unanswered questions as I re-entered the commotion of Rye Lane. The day was warming up. I felt a general sense of happiness and well-being that was also coming out of the crowd. The atmosphere felt so different from the grim, grey despair that had surrounded me during my studies

---

4   Simone de Beauvoir, *The Second Sex*. London: Joanathan Cape, 1960

in northern England at that time of Thatcherian implosion and economic freefall. Whatever the followers of Sheikh Nazim were doing in London, it was an improvement on that.

❖ ❖ ❖

When I first met her, Meryem with her husband, Selim, had moved Sheikh's London base from a decrepit mosque at Green Lanes, East Ham, London, into a slightly less decrepit and more imposing Victorian Gothic Revival church in Peckham financed by the Turkish Cypriot community. The population was alive and flourishing after having fled the events of the Cypriot upheaval during the 1960s and 1970s.

Meryem was a centre of gravity, the kind of woman who draws everyone toward her with her kindness and generosity. She was very maternal and gave the same love to the young people from Europe and America who came to visit her Sheikh that she gave to her family. Sheikh Nazim, and subsequently his followers, would take over her small home above the grocery shop during the fasting month of Ramadan, which the Sheikh always spent in London.

Meryem never complained about the disruption or the hardship of cooking enormous pots of Turkish stew to take to the fasting mureeds staying at the mosque every evening. She would greet people, ask them about their loved ones, listening to their troubles or triumphs with equanimity, often murmuring, "Alhumdulillah!"

The "Naqshbandi Ramadan Scene" was an annual event and "happening" for the followers of Sheikh Nazim for many years in the 70s and early 80s. He would arrive from Cyprus and then came the crowds: young and old and in between, rich and poor, distinct cultural groups reflecting the global village would pass through and camp out, fast and pray in unity. For me, it was a wonderful opportunity to spend time with the Sheikh and I could also stay at my mother's flat in North London.

Meryem's small front room, up a narrow flight of stairs beside the shop doorway, gradually lost all furniture over the years to make space for the people assembling there. Only a large armchair remained, like the one in the kitchen, for Sheikh to sit in and give his morning talk. There were two talks every day, and the first one took place at the shop around 11 a.m. It was a suitable time

15

to ask questions, and to get a private consultation with him if you had the right connections. Quickly, the number of people increased and toward the end of the "Peckham years," visitors blocked the stairs, as the living room was full, and sometimes the line would go out into the street. Minor celebrities would come to visit and consult the Sheikh, but the "important people" were able to get him and his large entourage to visit their luxurious homes for the "fast break," Iftar, the social event at sunset during the fasting month of Ramadan.

❖   ❖   ❖

Meryem's presence and influence on the Peckham scene were clear and consistent. She applied the traditional model of spiritual ascension for women, which was to be a pious and observant Muslim, a dutiful wife, and to serve her children and the rest of humanity in the most positive, practical way that she could.

Some years after we had started going on an annual visit from Montreal, we got the heartbreaking news that Ramadan in Peckham would no longer be happening. It was over. The implications of this for the North American mureeds were that they no longer had relatively easy access to him and his teachings. For Ibrahim and me, it was a huge and irrevocable loss.

Becoming Muslim,
First Visit to Cyprus

❧

I remembered my meeting with the Sheikh and kept a photo that Canadian Ibrahim had given me of them together next to the Volkswagen camper van. They are both smiling and looking relaxed and happy, in the background are green fields and snow-capped mountains. I kept it in my small address book, which I always had in case I needed to phone someone. I wanted to remember this extraordinary meeting that had changed my life.

However, Ibrahim was not the kind of seeker who moved on in the typical transient way of many global travellers. He started to send me letters and postcards from the former Yugoslavia, from Turkey, from Syria. One morning, my mum came into my room at her London flat and gave me a large white envelope with Syrian stamps on it. I recognized the sloped handwriting at once. In it, he detailed his experiences in a "Sufi village" somewhere in Kurdistan. He highly recommended that I come out and join him there. I was so shocked that I put it to one side. I wasn't sure of the reality that this person was living in. In the UK at that time, unemployment was at a record high and I had no money. I was in "survival mode."

Later, I did a gouache portrait of the Sheikh from memory and sent it to Ibrahim at his Canadian address. He replied promptly and very enthusiastically. We continued to keep in touch. When I reflected on the extraordinary Sheikh

Nazim, my time in Switzerland, and Canadian Ibrahim, it was like remembering a place far removed from the "ordinary" world. A "faraway land" where the harsh realities of daily struggle didn't intrude. My feelings for Ibrahim were also part of a special place in my heart where I kept them closed and cherished, protecting them from the complications of disenchantment and betrayal.

After some struggles and lots of applications, I had found the part-time job as a teacher at the East End of London school and a place to live in a shared house with adults with intellectual limitations in Islington. One evening, Ibrahim showed up unexpectedly at the MENCAP house where I lived on St. Paul's Road. He had got my address from my mother but did not have the phone number. I was surprised but happy about this unannounced visit.

My housemates were equally intrigued by this middle-aged man in full Naqshbandi regalia with a large beard. As adults with cognitive deficits, they had seen quite a few psychiatrists before, but never in this context and looking like this one. I awkwardly invited him down to my small basement room with a single bed, bean bag, and desk/drawers because we couldn't sit in the communal areas of the group home.

We talked late into the night about common interests, religion, psychology, mysticism, and other things. He missed the last tube train back to Meryem's, so he had to sleep on the sofa in the shared living room. I got up extra early before work the next day to try to get him out before the residents saw him, but he wanted to stay for breakfast. He talked about a dream he had about the Taj Mahal. I had good dreams also, but I didn't remember them. I made him some Nescafé and a slice of toast. I waved goodbye to him as he headed off down St Paul's Road. I felt sad to see him go. I imagined that he would go back to Canada and his patients and his life there, and I would continue with mine on the other side of the Atlantic.

A few months after his visit, I moved back to Switzerland again, this time for work. Michael had specifically asked me to move out there to his new headquarters in a posh suburb of Zurich. By that time, my teaching job no longer existed due to the strike, so I left my dear housemates in Islington and headed to Europe and to what seemed an extraordinary opportunity. The party started once again with the energy work and, as a member of the inner circle around Michael, each day was full of surprises and demands. I sent Ibrahim my new address, and he wrote several times, telling me about his challenges as a Jewish Muslim, his psychiatric research, and some more adventures on the Sufi path. Eventually, toward the end of a hot and intense Swiss summer, I got a letter saying he had a connecting flight through Zurich on his way to Istanbul. Would I like to meet him for a few hours and have lunch?

❖   ❖   ❖

Up until the day I went to meet Ibrahim at the airport, I was struggling with the decision. *Perhaps I should just ignore this crazy Sufi and his remarkable Sheikh?* I did not want to change my behaviour and "limit" myself and my own individualistic version of the "spiritual path." I was engaged with the New Age movement and the flourishing Wild Goose Company, which was one of the first to provide workshops and materials connected to specific teachers. There was no way at that point I wanted to become Muslim and exchange this free lifestyle for a conventional one. The collective around me in the large house of the start-up company was New Age and very liberal. I turned for advice to a wise older woman, one of the more practical and experienced people present, and told her a little about the letter, the sender and the invitation. She laughed.

"A handsome man has offered to meet you and buy you lunch? You don't know if you should go? Are you crazy? Of course, you should go!"

So, I went.

At Zurich airport, I waved to Ibrahim as he came into the light-filled reception area from the flight. I was wearing an all-white "boiler suit" with a blue and yellow belt around the waist. The height of fashion in our crowd at that time. He looked less inspired and more tired than I had seen him previously. He had just finished his psychiatric internship. Over a "snack" at the airport café, I shared my disappointment with the work and the company I was now part of. I had survived there for almost a year, which was quite remarkable given the bizarre company culture and Michael's unbridled narcissism and tantrums—the corruption and whispering plots that took place daily, the "power trips," and the greed and ostentation at the centre of it all. Michael had just bought a new Ferrari Testarossa for cash and meanwhile, the people working at the company were only receiving room and board.

Ibrahim sincerely invited me to go with him to visit the Sheikh. It was as if a door opened, and through it, I could see a beautiful garden in my mind. The "faraway land" was calling me once more. We rushed back on the tram to where I was staying, a rented house for the company workers, and quickly packed a bag of my essentials. I left a note saying goodbye to my housemates and quitting. It simply said, "I just can't stand any more of this bullshit. Sorry I didn't get the laundry soap and maybe B. can do the mailing list. Love."

We got back to the airport just in time to board the small, mostly empty plane to Turkey.

I remembered my friend's voice from the day before . . . *Are you crazy?*

"Yes, I am." I laughed to myself, full of joy for the first time in a long time.

We took off.

We stayed in Istanbul at the spacious apartment of a friend of Ibrahim's. He had just come back from making Hajj, the required pilgrimage to Mecca, which is one of the five pillars of Islam along with Shahada (faith), Salat (5 times prayer), Zakat (charity), Sawm (fasting). The friend had suitcases overflowing with purchases all around the luxurious living room of their apartment in Kadikoy.

Our generous host presented me with a fluorescent green polyester scarf with fringes. This may have been because his wife, who did not wear hijab, didn't want it. Neither did I, but I accepted it anyway, and it became very useful as I travelled through Turkey. By wearing this scarf, I was transformed from a foreign tourist to a young woman who was on a spiritual journey. Hijab at that time, the beginning of the 80s, was an unusual "fashion statement" and more. It was also telling a narrative that the lives of women like Meryem held fulfillment and contentment that was unavailable from pursuing career ambitions and assuming a traditional masculine mind set. I was starting to understand the way of the world around the Sheikh and appreciate that the Naqshbandi path was also a holistic world view that could penetrate every part of life.

As we travelled around Istanbul, Ibrahim in traditional Turkish peasant clothes and me in loose long shirts over pants and the green scarf, we met kindness and warmth wherever we went. Old ladies hugged me and gave me sweets. Families pressed us with invitations to their homes, and I drank so much tea that I had to visit the smelly latrines of the city often, always looking for toilet paper and regretting not bringing any, having to use a water jug instead.

After a week of exploring and discovering Istanbul, a departure from our generous and patient host was needed. There is an informal understanding that guests do not stay for more than three nights and we had overstayed that, so we boarded a bus to Konya. During the ride, Ibrahim explained the interconnection between Sufism and Islam.

When the first Sufi teachers, such as Hazrat Inayat Khan, came to the West, they changed "Sufism" to make it more palatable. The West didn't like Islam because it contradicted many of their modern values and beliefs. Sensing that there was a receptivity to a mystical inclusive message but not an Islamic one, the teachers sidelined Islam and replaced it with a vague moral sense, which among many followers simply didn't develop. This led to all kinds of confusion and misunderstanding as the groups merged with the hippy counterculture.

The West didn't understand Islam, often seeing it through the colonialist lens of backwardness and superstition. Ibrahim was the first one to explain to me that to make "real" spiritual progress, you had to be embodied and grounded. You had to live and work "in the world" and make a practical contribution to everyone in the society around you and your family. It was not based on individual choices but instead guidelines for human beings, which went back to the dawn of time. This was why it was so important to clear yourself of bad intentions and purify your thoughts to make space for "barakat." It was also important to connect with Allah and try to resist negative thoughts and evil actions, a process known as Jihad al-nafs.

In Konya, we shared a hotel room with two old single beds a few feet apart. It was the only room available and Ibrahim was concerned for my personal safety as a Western woman in a foreign country; he didn't want to put me in a single room alone. I thought nothing about sharing a room, having slept in dormitories in hostels and student lodgings. The only thing that surprised me was that Ibrahim didn't make any overtures toward me sexually and insisted that we both dress separately in the bathroom. He explained that this was part of his spiritual practice, which I later understood to mean controlling desires and emotions.

We took the ferry to Famagusta in "Turkish Cyprus," which at that time was not recognized as a part of Turkey by international agreement. I have always loved ferries and sea trips. We spent most of the time sitting on benches on the deck and a golden light hit the ancient port as we came in. By this time, we had been travelling together for over a week, and Ibrahim had made the travel plans and negotiated our interactions with others. He explained that he was referring to me as his wife because Turkey was a very conservative country, and they wouldn't appreciate a couple travelling together unless they were married.

I found this amusing, but there was also a part of me that enjoyed it, being taken care of and not having to assert myself and control things to try to make them "fair" or tolerable as I had to at previous times when I was travelling alone. It was relaxing and enjoyable to feel taken care of and protected.

We took a dusty taxi and finally arrived late afternoon in Lefke, the small Cypriot town where Sheikh Nazim had made his home. We passed by a large statue of Ataturk, which a pigeon had made a nest on top of. Lefke was a simple place. It was not a wealthy merchant or market town and not a tourist destination. At that time, it was not the hub of a huge movement, the many followers of Sheikh Nazim taking over the town. Many of the buildings were run down, in need of painting and repairs. The streets were very quiet because nearly all the young people and families had left for opportunities elsewhere, some to the cities on the island but a large part in a diaspora to the West.

The taxi drew up alongside an ancient wall made of large square blocks of stone and with two large wooden doors below an archway to the right. There was a smaller door inside one of them. Ibrahim got out and began knocking, then hammering, on the door calling, "As salaam Alaikum, Sheikh Nazim!" After some time, the door opened, and Sheikh appeared in the doorway. He greeted Ibrahim as a guest, and then he saw me standing in the background with my backpack.

"What is this?" he demanded to know.

My stomach sank, and I froze. *Had I made a huge mistake in coming all this way?*

"It's Jane! From Switzerland! You remember?" Ibrahim responded enthusiastically.

"Humph! New wife? What for then?"

He directed Ibrahim to go a few yards down the lane to the door that went into the tekke, where the other male mureeds went. Scowling, he turned to me. "You! Go in there."

A Faraway Place

❧

S heikh Nazim directed me to go through the small doorway he came out of into another extraordinary world.

The house had been a ruin from Ottoman times. Sheikh Nazim had bought the land and was carefully and slowly restoring it. The complex was three sides around a lush garden with jasmine pots, fruit trees, and palms. Smooth flagstones led to different rooms accessed through the outer area. The rooms, except those on the second floor of the main part, all faced the central court-yard garden, which was also a living area, with a kitchen table and benches and areas for different activities such as vegetable preparation which took place just outside the indoor cooking area. The combination of light honey-coloured stone, the flowers in clay pots, trees and fruits in the garden, and the simple wooden furniture were breathtaking in their simplicity and loveliness.

A bohemian-styled woman introduced herself as I was standing there, wondering what I was supposed to do. "Hi, my name is Amatullah," she said in German-accentuated English. This was a huge relief because the situation I left in Switzerland was full of German people just like this. Here was someone who wouldn't be appalled by my recent travel arrangements. She pointed out the Sheikh's youngest daughter, Rashida, who at that time was around fifteen, and Asma, a young married woman who also lived with them. I did not meet the Sheikh's wife for a while, perhaps because she was too shy or busy, but after the daughter had described me, she came to meet me. Later, I would also meet

Rabia, a brilliant German Jewish woman who spoke several languages fluently and had transcribed and published the Sheikh's first books, the "Mercy Ocean" series. My gratitude toward these wonderful people who helped and welcomed me is limitless. They were truly sent by Allah to guide me at the right time.

We slept at a large building on the edge of town, which had been purchased as a guest house to accommodate the travellers who were coming to meet Sheikh more and more often.

The next time Sheikh Nazim appeared, it was at his home, and I was sitting on a bench outside the kitchen. He didn't want to talk about Islam or why I was there. Instead, he wanted to talk about the trip.

"Where did you stay in Istanbul?"

I told him the name of the friend who had hosted us in Istanbul.

He nodded curtly. Only later did I realize why Ibrahim had been referring to me as his wife and the implications of our journey together. It was a bad reflection not only on Ibrahim but also on his mureed, recognizable by his distinctive dress, to travel with a young, single woman who was neither his wife nor a near relative.

Public consensus in conservative circles was very harsh, and any suggestion of casual liaisons outside of marriage was not acceptable to the social standards. Once your status and reputation were harmed, it was almost impossible to get it back. Sheikh Nazim was acutely aware of that, and Westerners coming from urban areas were not. Our own internal morality has replaced the old traditional morality of villages and religious groups, but Sheikh ran in a different zone where religious law and the interpretations of religious scholars and jurists were how things were decided.

Sheikh Nazim's reputation had to be impeccable within the small group of religious leaders around in Syria, Egypt, and elsewhere. The behaviour and Adab (or courtesy, also closely circumscribed) of people associated with him were considered a reflection of his spiritual authority. I intuited this, as it reminded me of villages I visited in Wales, and so I mostly understood the expectations of the context. Many of the female and male mureeds did not, however, and this became a huge area of conflict for the tariquat (Sufi lineage following a sheikh) as a whole. "Westerners" versus "traditionalists," as time played out.

My friend Amatullah went back to Germany, and now I was the only Western woman at the guest house. The fact that three people of different genders were living together in a house on the edge of the village may have been put under the category of "wild Western followers" by the locals and perhaps the Sheikh's family. The two men were Ibrahim and "Crazy Abdullah," who was nicknamed this because of his erratic behaviour and psychiatric diagnosis. Despite this name, he frequently came out with insightful and pertinent explanations about the Sufi path and the methods of wayfaring it. He had become a semi-permanent resident in the village, having travelled extensively in India, Pakistan, and Iran, meeting Sufi Sheikhs. The three of us had the house to ourselves.

Another day, sitting in the garden at the Sheikh's house, I just burst into tears. My unease and insecurity as an outsider in this new, guarded world were overwhelming me. I had already been through so much in my life and I was unable to adapt to the relaxation and "no pressure" ease of the situation. Every time I got up to help, I was told to sit. I was a "guest" and so should just sit and be served. So, I just sat on the bench, looking at the garden for hours and hours. This was a lot harder than it might sound. Once I had stopped moving, my inner agitation surfaced. My "monkey mind," activated by change and trauma, was scanning the environment the whole time, on alert for danger. I felt I had to prove my worthiness at every opportunity; otherwise, I would be "fired," excluded, or expelled. That had been my experience growing up with a widowed mother who was unable to manage any aspect of her life, and it had led to constant rejection and displacement as she "burned bridges" and people along the way.

"They are beating you?" Sheikh asked with his head slightly on one side.

The thought of sweet, gentle Hajja Amina beating anyone, even a carpet, made me smile. I didn't know why the tears, but looking back, it appears that the innocence and simplicity of the situation were extraordinary and quite unlike anything I had been in. These women were protected and coddled. They were not supposed to worry about their domestic situation and instead trusted the leaders and elders of their community to decide and do things for them. This reality worked very well for centuries, but it did not work for me growing up in London or for any women that I know of growing up now. Perhaps the rise of feminism and self-assertion is also linked to this, as people struggle more and more as individuals, without anchors or roots or established paths for their lives. Modern life has become even more difficult to negotiate, and many people now struggle to provide themselves with the necessities of housing and food.

Western women believed that by staying on the "women's side" in this world, they were somehow "missing out." The tension increased over the coming years as more and more "Western" women refused to go there and instead went to the tekke with the men. On the women's side, Sheikh was accessible when he came through the doorway in the garden wall. It was important to be respectful that this was also his family time and not bother him with too many questions. In the company of his family, he was much more relaxed and often stayed there longer. It was a privilege to be there, and I was always careful to follow the lead and behaviours of the other women.

❖   ❖   ❖

"Pass me my turban," he muttered without looking at me.

No one else was around, and it was sitting on the table next to him. I looked at it and was not sure how to continue. After a second or so, I gently pinched the green peak between my thumb and forefinger of my right hand and lifted it. It was surprisingly heavy. Was that just the weight of the light Muslin wrapped around it, or was it something more? I put my other hand under the brim to steady and support it because dropping it and watching the fabric unravel would have been awful. I handed it to him. He nodded and, taking it with both hands, put it on his head like a crown. Then he walked off.

I felt then that I belonged in the tariquat.

The love was there and nothing in the way of it.

The Journey to the Heart

༺

The Sufis talk about the journey to the heart. By the heart, they mean the mystical centre where God and humanity unite. The most tangible corporate reality of our relationship with the divine. The evidence of this reality and the presence of God in our lives is our experience of love. Pure love in all its aspects, from the blossoming of flowers to the sacrifice of our lives for the good of others.

There are veils over our heart. Each loss, each time the connections that we have with others are cut, we lose a part of our hearts. I did not have the love of others to sustain me. I had lost my family and the places I had loved where I felt whole, like in Wales, where my grandfather had lived before he died. "Heartbreak" was a constant in my life. My heart had become so veiled that it had become "walled off."

At Sheikh's house and during my time sitting on the bench in the garden, I began to see the obstacles on the way back to love that prevented me from simple human interaction. I was full of grief, fear, and disappointments. I had been exposed to much negativity and corruption; I could no longer connect with people in a deeper way. I drifted toward those with whom I felt "safe," and I felt that being with Sheikh's family. I saw the simple, loving, everyday interactions that they had with one another, and it was astonishing to me.

There were no "games" (in the Eric Berne sense, *Games People Play*), no transactions (in a capitalist way), no negotiations, no resentments, no silences, no "offences taken," and no blame and shame dished out. In the societies that I knew, every interaction was fraught with these, whether it was within middle-class English society or New Age group development workshops. Everyone was "carrying a burden of baggage" that prevented them from simply being with another.

Here is an example. Ibrahim had given me a book, gifted to his Sheikh by one of the Turkish mureeds called *The Essentials of Islam*.[5] It was a straightforward guide to the basics of becoming a practising Muslim, written and translated into English with a clear style and practical chapters on topics like "Making wudu" and "The Five Daily Prayers." It also contained text and transcriptions of Ayats from the Quran as well as duah (Individual prayers in Arabic).

I was studying the book carefully in preparation for embracing Islam, saying the Shahadah in front of Muslim witnesses. I carried it everywhere, and with a lot of "free time" on my hands, I frequently took it out, studied a bit and then put it down to come back to later. One day, I had been trying to memorize one of the Ayats in transliteration while sitting in the prayer room of the house. It was a lovely, raised room with double doors that opened out onto the garden. The floor was covered in Turkish kilims. It was wonderfully tranquil, full of light and peace, the perfect spot for reading. When the Azan was called, I put the book down to go and stand beside Rashida, to imitate her movements, as I was doing in those days. After the prayer, I went back into the garden and forgot about my book. When it was time to go back to the guest house, I looked for the book everywhere, but I couldn't find it.

After I had checked my room at the guest house, just in case I had become confused and left it there, the next day I asked Rashida if she had seen it. She shook her head.

Later, she came and explained that I had left the book in the prayer room. She pointed at the place in the corner where I had been sitting reading it. I nodded, but why was the book not there? Then Hajja Amina appeared and, through Rashida, explained that the book had been face down on the floor. It held Ayats from the Quran, and I had been disrespectful.

I found this mind blowing. This was a book, an ordinary material object as far as I was concerned. This was not literally a "holy item." In my world, there was a distinct separation between the spiritual and the everyday world, and books

---

5   M.H. Kamali *The Essentials of Islam. Turkey, 1983 published privately*

were an item like any other. All my life, I had been fortunate enough to have books, and all my life, I had left them carelessly lying around. I had a habit of reading and then, lacking a bookmark, leaving them open on the page and then propping them up like a tent so that I could return to them and quickly pick up where I had left off. This is what I had done with this book.

It was only returned to me when I made a solemn vow to not treat it like that, and for the rest of my life, I have been careful and conscious about the way that I treat books. Smiling lightly, Hajja Amina handed the book over. The most significant part of this whole incident was, however, the ramifications. There weren't any. There was no mention of it going forward. It was erased. The slate was wiped clean. We were back in the sea of the golden light. Love was always there, like the sun, even when the clouds hid it.

٭ ٭ ٭

The knowledge of the presence of love is the secret at the heart of the Naqshbandi tariquat. I found an explanation—I don't know if it's "true"—in a book by a contemporary Sufi Sheikha, Mrs. Irina Tweedie, in her book, *Chasm of Fire (U.K., Element books, 1979)*. In India, the Naqshbandis are known as the Golden Sufis because the pure colour of the enlightened heart is gold. Like the expression, heart of gold. And the true mureeds and followers of the Sheikhs have this, a heart of gold. The connections that are made around a true Sheikh are deep and lasting; they are rooted in and nourished by this divine love. They have a constant "fertilizer bath" of spiritual nourishment. The reality is our hearts need support because, as humans, we simply cannot do this by ourselves. Our bodies and "lower self" (nafs) become conditioned by our negative experiences, and they become the blueprint for how we go on to interact with the world. Within the tariquat, even though these are there, we can transcend the scripts and conditions because we have a constant stream of pure love in which to bathe ourselves and wash away all the heartbreak and "thousand natural shocks that flesh is heir to".

It was in this 'love field' that Ibrahim and I were able to connect and form a bond that is lifelong. I was able to open my heart, and so could he. The secret to our being together, despite our personalities, our neurosis, and our woundedness, was this connection, going back to the source like the sun.

The Marriage

୬

There was a shocking joke in the Naqshbandis that choosing a bride was like choosing a sheep. You had to check the teeth and the rump; a healthy size and no teeth missing. Maybe the similarity didn't just end with a wedding ceremony but went as far as the sacrifice. The marriages in the tariquat were a large part of the experience of initiation and membership because the structure was based, as traditional Muslim cultures are, on family units and the ceremonies around them.

One day during this first visit, Rashida took me into the simple kitchen at the house. She explained that she, her mother and Sheikh were travelling to Girne for an overnight stay and so would not be able to make food for the mureeds at the guest house—at that time, Ibrahim, Abdullah, and myself. So, it would be my responsibility. As I had grown up cooking, I felt confident, but it was very important that this was Turkish food, which I was not familiar with.

With great care, she showed me how to make stuffed aubergines. This is a traditional Turkish dish; there are many stuffed vegetables in the cuisine. I bought the fresh ingredients from the local market and followed her instructions diligently, pre-cooking the aubergine a little, and incorporating some of the inside flesh into the meat, tomato, and vegetable filling. Later, I adapted the recipe, pouring the tomato and meat on top of the aubergine, baking it, and serving on a bed of rice.

It was a culinary triumph. Abdullah and Ibrahim gazed at me when they finished their second helpings.

"You mean this is the recipe of the daughter of the Sheikh? This recipe has the Sunnah of the Sheikh's family! This is a holy recipe!" declared Abdullah.

Abdullah, always great at domestic tasks, began to get busy with the dishes. He used a two-bowl method, one to soap and one to rinse, which used less water, which there was not much of in Cyprus.

Ibrahim met my eyes and insisted we "go for a walk." We went through the empty streets to a dark and silent mosque in the village centre. When I sat down on the stone steps at the front of the mosque, Ibrahim gallantly went down on one knee and asked me to be his wife.

With joy and gratitude and a little relief, I accepted. He had brought me to the Sheikh, Islam, and the Naqshbandi Way. He was the most brilliant man I had ever met, handsome, charismatic, and professionally trained in a medical field I had always found fascinating. He was more than I had ever hoped for or expected to share my life with.

❖ ❖ ❖

Although I had been told more than once that I was "intended" for Dr. Ibrahim, there had been no overtures on his part, and I was concerned about what I should do. I could not see a way to still be in this context as a single woman, although later on, several Western women did.

In the next days Hajja Amina would say, "Dr. Ibrahim is a good man," and I would agree.

Sheikh Nazim would ask, "Dr. Ibrahim, he is all right for you?"

And I would agree.

I had a suit made by the ladies' dressmaker in the village, who measured me and clucked because I had a large waist. Ibrahim went to the tailor and had a blue and white striped gallabiyah made. The wedding would take place the following week at Jumaah.

❖ ❖ ❖

The Hammam

The only indoor plumbing in the guest house was the tap in the kitchen. One morning, I heard some voices outside and spotted Sheikh Nazim right there in the back area with a group of men around him and a cement mixer.

Abdullah was very excited. "Our glorious Sheikh is building a Hammam, and it will be for you, for your wedding! You need to be cleansed in every way. We need to remove the filth of the West from you and make you a pure and whole woman again."

Although I found this comment rather strange, I understood that Abdullah had been immersed in Muslim traditional culture for many years and subsequently, he had picked up some of the prejudice against women from more liberal environments.

The contributions of Abdullah had often been very helpful. We would share a snack and tea at the small wooden table in the guest house in Lefke as he didn't do the reflexive action of male mureeds: avoid all women and not talk to them. I appreciated the valuable information and cultural nuggets he shared with me, as much of the time, I had no idea what was happening. He managed everyday life in Cyprus very well, especially the outdoor latrine. Instead of smelling like a barn, it was pleasant and clean with his daily maintenance. The secret he shared was to pour kerosene down it and then add a lighted rag every week or so. He had learned that somewhere on his extensive travels.

It was early on Friday morning of my wedding day, and I looked at the red plastic bucket on the floor of the newly built Hammam facility. "I have prepared it for you, and you will have complete privacy for your ablution!" Abdullah assured me. The smell of drying cement was still present, and I heard the crackle of some sticks burning somewhere inside one of the walls. They weren't doing a very good job of heating it, and I couldn't imagine how I was going to take a steam bath or even a bath at all. I had been instructed to take a full shower and remove every hair on my body by one of the local women at the tailors.

Not every hair, surely, I thought. Armed with a plastic razor borrowed from the groom, a bar of Lux soap, and a small bottle of green shampoo, I decided I would start with my legs and then do the hair wash at the end, hoping that the small chamber would have warmed up. It seemed to have become colder by the time

I rinsed off the shampoo. It was necessary to dry myself quickly before putting on the light blue jacket and skirt that the tailor had made. The style was chosen from a catalogue in her room in the village. I wanted to wear it later as well.

I walked down the lane to Sheikh's house, feeling some fears about how this marriage would go and the future in general. Muslim men have the right to marry up to four women, and I had made Ibrahim promise that he would not take another wife without consulting me. The "modern" argument for this practice was that sometimes wives became sick or were unable to have children. I had met a German convert family where there were two wives, and the older one had agreed to a younger, second wife so that they could both have the joy of raising a child together. I had found the idea appalling and reassured myself with the model of Sheikh's family. His lovely home and devoted wife, loving children who were now almost all adults. It seemed such a great and harmonious blessing.

One of the women of the family, Asma, offered to lend me her make-up, so I sat in a chair in her bedroom and put on L'Oréal mascara that probably came from Lebanon when she had, may Allah bless her. We had some wedding soup that Hajja Amina had made for breakfast, and I sat and waited in the garden next to an ancient woman with a creased face and wrinkled mouth. She gazed at me.

"I was the most beautiful bride in the village, and I married the most hand-some man. I had two sons and two daughters, and now they have all gone away. My husband is dead, and now I am old and alone."

I looked at her, and after a while, something in me said, ". . . and one day I will be just like you," and she looked into my eyes, and I got goosebumps up and down my spine. When she laughed, it was like a dark hole opened in her face. Rashida told me that that woman was a wali and that I was very blessed that she had come to visit. Her message was a reminder.

One of the male mureeds had brought the van around to the front door and the ladies all climbed in the back for the trip to open a new mosque and Salat al Jummah, Friday prayer. Hajja Amina had put up little curtains on wires, either for privacy or sun protection, but we did not draw them and I sat next to the window. It was nice to look outside, although it was bumpy and there were no seat belts. It seemed like a long drive to Nicosia.

At one point on the trip, Ibrahim turned around, looked at me, and frowned. He didn't like the grey and red scarf I was wearing; he did not think it matched the blue. One of my first actions as his wife was to take it off while keeping my hair hidden and slip on the white one in my backpack. I had no pin, so I sort of wrapped it. He smiled and gave me a loving look.

There was a largish crowd of men in dark slacks, shirts, and ties and they looked like businesspeople for the Friday collective prayer. A decent crowd for a Jumaah prayer, but there was no one and nothing in the women's section. There was, however, a kind of grill on one side, which let the light in and through which we could see the men's side and the Sheikh.

We sat on the floor and we waited. I was getting used to doing that by this point. I did not know how this ceremony would happen, so I was anxious. Hajja Amina smiled and patted a cushion next to her for me to sit down on. For that day, she was my Muslim mother. My actual mother was back in London, recovering from her latest health crisis and probably watching telly. I had invited her at the last minute to come to Cyprus; to my relief, she had demurred. I couldn't imagine her functioning in this context, anyway.

Sheikh Nazim called me over to the ornate wooden grill. All the men gathered around him and peered at me. A largish man with curly hair stood closest. "I am a professor at the London School of Economics, and I will be your wakeel, your representative." I had no idea what that meant. There was a discussion away from me in the middle of the room.

Then, Sheikh appeared back at the grill. "Repeat after me," he said.

I tried hard to remember each syllable as he said it, which required a lot of concentration. I wasn't familiar with either Arabic or Turkish. I said the Shahada, my testimony of faith in Islam. **Transliteration:** *"Ash-hadu an la ilaha illa Allah, Wa ash-hadu anna Muhammadan Rasulu-Allah."*

Translation: "I bear witness that there is no God but God (Allah), and Muhammad is the Messenger of Allah."

Sheikh Nazim poked a miswaq (tooth stick) through a hole in the grill, and I stared at it, and then someone said to touch the other end. More repetition for Bayaat. (Initiation into the Naqshbandi Tariquat)

More talking amongst the men. I heard later that as Sheikh didn't know my father's name, I was described as "A daughter of Adam." I tried to get Ibrahim's attention, but he was busy taking photographs. We would later have a set of photos of random men sitting around on a cement floor.

I turned around to ask Rashida how I would get to the men's side for the ceremony. She lifted her eyes in surprise then she said, "Oh, that was it. Congratulations."

Just then, Sheikh Nazim raised his hands and started off on a long duah. He was talking loudly and rapidly, sounding like he was angry. I cowered inside. Perhaps he'd had an intuition of the kind of thing I was doing before I became Muslim, and maybe he had to do a sort of exorcism. Sheikh continued on, I heard the word "Shaitain" (devil). I was full of fear that my new spiritual teacher had realized just how sinful and awful I was. I felt like I had been acting like a hypocrite so far. In my heart, I repented, saying "EstfirAllah," over and over silently.

Outside the mosque, just after the wedding. August 1985

After Sheikh Nazim had finished the long duah, I was able to find Ibrahim, and as we stepped outside the mosque, I raised my eyes to look at the street, and it was as if a curtain, a veil, was lifted up. Underneath it was light on light that had always been there, creating, manifesting, drawing back, living eternal. Always there behind our usual perception, that same light witnessing itself, the veil being lifted, reconnecting and joining with everything. Then, as I was staring at small grey clouds gathering in the sky just above us, I felt raindrops on my face, and then they splattered on my blue suit and the dusty ground beneath. The men in the street cried "Mashallah!" and danced with joy—not for the wedding or the new mosque, but because that long duah that Sheikh had been making in the mosque had been for rain. There was a severe drought in Cyprus, and now it was raining, just in a particular spot in Nicosia. The light, the Nour, was sending the blessing of rain, which is considered a lovely and refreshing thing which brings life. The harsh, choking dust settled, and we were sprinkled and refreshed. I was cleansed and reborn on that day as a mureed, a wife, and a Muslim, and I witnessed a miracle. I was also given the Muslim name of Munirah.

Before we left Cyprus, Sheikh Nazim spoke with us. He asked Ibrahim and me to go back to Canada, work together and build the Naqshbandi tariquat. As usual, he was going somewhere, and the meeting was rushed and impromptu. I had a sense that we had had "our time" and we should move on quickly now to let him get on with more important business. Ibrahim was always good at getting Sheikh's attention, though, and this time, when he did, I rushed over, pushing my way through the gaggle of men around so that I could stand next to Ibrahim. This had become my only way to get anywhere near Sheikh when I wasn't with the other women and he was in a public space.

"You will go back to Canada, buy land, and plant fruit trees. You will meet people and invite them to Islam. You will do dhikr every week and go to the mosques. Make dawah (the Islamic term for inviting others to Islam), and people will come."

So, this became our mission statement. I would be the homemaker, mother, and host, and Ibrahim would be Sheikh's representative in Canada. The model of a rural agricultural Sufi commune was already working in Germany. There was one already in North America Dar al Islam,[6] in New Mexico, USA. It was not a Naqshbandi initiative though but we would go and visit to find out more.

---

6   "Dar al Islam in New Mexico," *Toronto Star*, July 31, 1999. https://hwpi.harvard. edu/pluralismarchive/news/dar-al-islam-new-mexico.

The Muslimah Who Fell to Earth

꙰

I arrived at Mirabel Airport, Quebec, Canada, in the last week of December 1985. It was a lofty, light-filled white albatross of a place in the middle of snowy white fields too far from Montreal.

I got to customs, a small white British girl wearing a grey duffle coat with a Turkish kerchief on her head. My passport was stamped full . . . Europe, Turkey, Cyprus, India, Syria, Greece, Bulgaria and other places. I had been a Muslim for six months, and had taken Shahada and Bayaat, a pledge of allegiance to my Sheikh of the Naqshbandi tariquat and got married all on the same day. There wasn't a marriage certificate because I had a Turkish Sufi wedding in Nicosia, Cyprus, which wasn't even recognized as a state at that time.

Welcome to Canada! Big Sky! Ibrahim is gorgeous! He was wearing a big fur hat with his bushy beard and warm brown eyes. He looked like a teddy bear . . . and about bears . . . yes, there is snow, but I didn't see any polar bears out of the car window on the drive back to Park Extension. I met Davy, my new father-in-law, who had come to collect his son's new bride. He was a little perplexed by his eldest son going to Jerusalem and then coming back a Sufi Muslim. His son's long spiritual journey had been even more confusing despite his Bar Mitzvah. Davy couldn't see why he didn't just settle down and make money like everyone else.

After we arrived at the family duplex, I met Sylvia, my mother-in-law. She was wearing a coral pink velvet jogging suit and had come home from her second job. She didn't like to sit still; she thought it lazy. She was a clever woman with strong opinions about almost everything. She reserved judgment on me, the new wife. I knew that statistics were not on the side of a long-term marriage, but I decided this marriage was going to be different because it was built on the rock of the tariquat and the traditions of the Naqshbandi, rather than modern individualism and fleeting emotions.

I, like Sylvia, kept my thoughts and concerns to myself. With Allah's grace, a miracle took place. We became friends, and my husband's family became my Canadian family, for which I am forever grateful. Disparate elements, different worlds. Through the wisdom of the heart, we came together, Subhanallah.

A month after my arrival, Ibrahim and I moved into our first home together. We rented a semi-detached cottage in the Town of Mont Royal with a basement for Ibrahim to see some of his patients. The rest of the week, he was at the Douglas Hospital. We started the first dhikr group in Montreal. The Sufis of TMR, a disparate bunch of adventurous spirits who would go on to become one of the foundations of Islamic Sufism in Canada. Our weekly dhikr became the focus of our practice and because we met together at our home, we referred to it as "the Sufi centre." The two mosques in Montreal would not tolerate a "Sufi" practice, which they considered highly suspect. The Naqshbandi is a major spiritual order of Sufism and one of many, but it is the only Sufi order that connects its chain of transmission back to Abu Bakr Siddiq, R.A., the first caliph of Islam and successor to Prophet Muhammad (PBUH). It was named after Shah Naqshbandi and came through Samarqand down to Damascus, where it was learned by our teacher, Sheikh Nazim. As well as Sufis, we were orthodox Sunni Muslims following the Hanafi madhhab (school of jurisprudence).

At that time, the Wahabis, as they were known by some, were funding almost all the dawah, Imam training, and foundations of Islam in Canada, it seemed. This puritanical and intolerant sect, which originated in Najd, Saudi Arabia, in the eighteenth century, was the version of Islam followed by the rulers of Saudia Arabia. They were responsible for financially supporting many of the mosques and Muslim organizations around the world. From this financial and educational control, their limited interpretation took over, unrecognized by many North American Muslims as anything but "the way it should be." Everything, except what they said, was "kufr, bida, or shirk" . . . especially Sufis, who, they claimed, worshipped dead bodies.

My first visit to the Islamic Centre of Quebec for Jummah prayer was during a blizzard. New to winter in Quebec, I didn't understand "more snow," "less snow," "freezing rain," "drifting snow road conditions," and so on. To me, it was all fun, a wonderful contrast to damp, dark London. So, I took the bus. I figured out the change, but when I waved my Montreal map with a large X marked on Grenet Street in Ville St Laurent at the driver, I think I must have startled him.

Although, at that time, terrorists were Irish, Montreal bus drivers were uniquely Quebecois, and their multi-cultural education was limited. He was very unfriendly.

Despite my smart shalwar kameez and my tuque turban, I even spoke French: "Excusez- moi, est-ce cet autobus va à la mosque?"

He angrily told me to get to the back of the bus.

Fortunately, a kind-hearted woman pointed out the window when my stop was coming. In that incarnation, the Islamic Centre of Quebec, ICQ as it is still known, was a long, low building with a homemade minaret on top that looked like a dented crocus bulb. As women were not allowed through the front door— "Estfirallah, sister"—I trudged through a snowbank to get around the back to a fire exit, which had a "Ladies" decal on it. Someone had thoughtfully wedged a rubber slipper in it so we could get in.

Once inside, the familiar feel of wet carpeting meeting dry sock and a waft of curry and synthetic jasmine perfume assured me that I was in the right place. The few Muslim sisters that were there were mostly unresponsive to my enthusiastic Salaams and affectionate hand clasping and kissing, which I had learned elsewhere. I thought I heard mumbled things about "Britishers," although one did ask, "Where are you from?" because I discovered, she had had a layover at Heathrow Airport on her way here and snacked on British candy bars.

I realize now that my "Turkish neo-Naqshbandi hybrid" and what they "learned back home about Islam" were diametrically opposed. For many of the women who bravely came to this cold, distant country, Islam was marriage, children, and martyrdom, with a bit of tajweed and samosas on special occasions. Many of them lived in Purdah not necessarily by choice but because they simply had no idea about how society functioned and no contact with the people around them in case they were "corrupted." If they spoke English, they did not speak French, they had no independent income and lived in apartment buildings in dangerous areas where, yes, you had better avoid your neighbours in case you were mugged.

I was very privileged. I had been mentored in Islam by the family of my wonderful Sheikh and now I had a "fresh start" from my punk post-modernist ways in the frozen wonderland of Canada. We had delicious food and lots of it, warm, well-built housing and appliances. Best of all I had a brilliant Sufi psychiatrist as my husband.

The psychic and spiritual wonders I had already seen connected to traditional Islam—like the Shrine of Kwaja Moinuddin Christi in Ajmer, India, and the Naqshbandi tekke in Damascus—were radically different from that which prevailed in the close-knit and very pious Muslim community of Montreal. Perhaps it was that the few thousand practising Muslims were too insecure to be tolerant at that time, but it was also the very narrow interpretation of the sunnah of our Prophet Muhammad as well as restricted access to Koranic translations and interpretations that met the narrow definition of what was acceptable to the new community. A painted toenail here and a slice of Saputo cheese there, and you would lose your balance on the Sirat al-Mustiqueem, falling into hellfire, along with many other residents of Quebec. There were enforcers everywhere. This was already widespread in some other countries. Usually at the mosque, but sometimes in the segregated "women's section" of community meetings, they would start with a hiss ... "Sister, it is my duty to tell you that a) your hair is showing or b) you closed your eyes during Salat c) your pronunciation of 'ha' is not aspirated, etc." ... If they had ever got inside the Sufi centre and seen the small photo of our Sheikh on the mantelpiece, it would have been enough to send them into paroxysms of rage ... "Harramm! You must re-do all your prayers and renounce this shirk!"

However, besides this unfortunate and vocal minority, there were some wonderful and caring women I also met at that time. There was a genuine opening of hearts, love, and friendship extended to me unconditionally. One of them was the first French Canadian woman I had ever met. She had survived a brutal upbringing in rural Quebec, escaped across Canada, and after some time in Vancouver, had returned to Montreal with her three-year-old daughter. When I met her, she had just married a Syrian-born engineer, and we were both expecting our first child as Muslim mothers. When she comes to mind, I see her in her homemade striped jellaba and a long white headscarf. She was the only woman I knew in Montreal who went freely around dressed like that. She introduced me to St Hubert Street, where we loved to shop for cheap bolts of fabric, and she gave me an English cookbook of Middle Eastern cooking. Together, we looked through the English translation of Al-Bukhari, Sahih (Hadith), Bukhara, 846a.d. and Imam Al-Ghazali's Ihyâ' 'ulûm al-dîn (The Revival of the Religious Sciences) Persia, 12 century- a standard textbook of Islamic knowledge. Her husband had requested her not to read anything else except these and *Chatelaine*.

Another dear friend came to Canada as a child from a refugee camp, and eighteen at the time, was married and expecting her first baby also. Later, her large son was a contrast to my small daughter at our dhikr meetings. As Sheikh Nazim had said, people gradually started to come. They were mostly young and well educated and searching for something deeper than the belief system of the 80s and previous generations. These deep connections were made on subtle levels, with hearts open to possibilities and invisible worlds of angels and miracles. Islam in North America was taking root and then blossoming. What could possibly go wrong?

Then there were the Quebecers, other than my good friend in her homemade outfits. They would carefully explain to me that although my husband was a third-generation Montrealer, he was not really a Quebecer because, to use Mordechai Richler's famous phrase, he was "impure wool." This ironic term was invented by the author as a response to the Quebecois traditionalist promotion of the "*pur laine*" culture of the earliest white settlers in Quebec. On the plus side, some old men would open doors for me, thinking I was a nun, and older women would curtsey and genuflect, especially when I visited St Joseph's Oratory, which I liked to do because of the vibes. Looking down from the top of the oratory over Montreal on a sunny day, it was clear that almost everything of value that had been done in the society and culture laid below was done by a Christian inclination and an army of priests and nuns. Besides which, the monks still made the best cheese and had the nicest real estate. It was hard for me to understand why the citizens of Montreal backed away at the mention of religion like vampires from garlic. The division of Church and State was something I took for granted; the Anglican Church had little influence on anything in modern Britain. There weren't any new theocratic states spouting Islamist sound bites to terrify the populations worldwide and in their countries. The war against Islam was not on the agenda. We were living like children in a state of innocence and enthusiastic love for our newfound alternative way of living. This was a grand beginning and, of course, inevitably, there would be a fall from Eden.

A year later, Ibrahim and our young family moved out to the Eastern Townships to start what we imagined would be the "Back to the land Sufi community," and a short while later, when we moved back to Montreal, I considered myself a veteran of the Canadian way of life. Older and wiser, I no longer felt like an alien. When I walked into the halal butcher shop on Decarie, I could buy all the "foul mesdames" and lamb shanks I needed, as well as spices and the all-important Patak's pickles to go with them. I was home, safe, and amongst friends and joined with the Ummah and the tariquat. We should have braced ourselves for the times that lay ahead.

❖ ❖ ❖

The Role of the Traditional Wife

How my role as a Muslim wife would unfold for me personally was another matter. I vividly remember one morning when the mureeds were sitting crowded in the reception room above Selim's shop in London. This was difficult because I was heavily pregnant with my first child. The room was filled with many mureeds and visitors who had arrived for Sheikh's morning talk. It was the first week of Ramadan, although I wasn't fasting because Sheikh Nazim and Ibrahim had both recommended to "make up the fast later"—after pregnancy and breast feeding. Motivated by this chance to bond with the wider Muslim community, I had camped out at Peckham Mosque and doggedly trailed after Sheikh Nazim and his family wherever they went. Ibrahim had arrived from Montreal and was sitting at the Sheikh's feet with his tape recorder. Sheikh Nazim was "patting them," metaphorically, giving them lots of positive energy, pumping them up like any good coach for the marathon fast ahead of them. Then, it was Ibrahim's turn for some special attention.

"Mashallah, big doctor, chief of crazy house and with new wife Munirah, alhumdullilah," Sheikh said, smiling and nodding his head approvingly, as if to imply, well done, that was quick. We had been married for less than a year. Then he stated, "Inshallah, Munirah has babies every year! Like a rabbit! Ten babies, twelve babies!" He chuckled, and the other mureeds and a couple of the women were smiling and nodding.

"You hear that?" one of them said, leaning in too close. "Sheikh is ordering you; you must do it. Have a baby every year," and she looked at me very pointedly. I did not like the way that this woman had spun what might have been a suggestion or a prediction into a fatwa and fate—Sheikh has said so; therefore, you must do it or be damned. That was not the way I interpreted the sayings of the Sheikh and never would. I shook my head. *No, this is some sort of Turkish joke, it must be, and I don't find it funny.*

Right there in that crowded room, I promised myself that it was not going to happen. Ibrahim and others could say it was my nafs (lower self) talking, the rebellious part of me, but also it was a survival instinct, and somehow, I knew I had to listen to it.

In Sufism, we struggle against the lower desires of our nature to overcome their hold on our psyche and "free up space" for the divine to enter our hearts. Subsequently, the nafs may be considered bad, and all the drives and desires associated with it are sometimes lumped into this process. Over time, I have come to respect my lower self and animal instincts, however. When we shut ourselves off from their instinctual and intuitive wisdom, there is a subsequent loss of vitality and purpose in our lives. If I wanted to have a huge family of children, perhaps the comments of Sheikh might have been received more positively by me, but I didn't.

Being pregnant and the limitations and struggles of motherhood are a huge burden for any modern woman, and the model was just not appropriate. I knew that multiple babies and the domestic toil associated with that were not where my strengths were. A year or two ago I would have been willing to embrace life-long celibacy and the loss of family life to reach Buddhist enlightenment. Now, I was a Sufi wife and mother, and I decided that after this baby, I would have "done my role," and I was anxious to get on with what I considered the "real" spiritual work without crying babies and sinks full of dishes. That was how I saw it; it was one path or another. I hadn't got to the place where I realized that you could make a very intense spiritual life out of everyday chores and service. In my mind, I still believed that you couldn't be a wife and mother and have much of a spiritual and intellectual life. I was misguided in that belief, but I also think that is a common one for many women.

It was during the same visit that another discordant note crept into my vision of service of the Sheikh. Over a year after my first visit to Meryem, I was pregnant, wearing a hijab, and chopping vegetables myself in her kitchen in Rye Lane. I had strategized that the best way to get access to my spiritual guide was by making myself useful in the kitchen where he was staying. I was also "camping out" with a few other women at the improvised international hostel of Peckham Mosque.

As I washed and chopped out the rotten bits from a mound of vegetables Selim had produced from the shop, I hoped for a chance to see Sheikh. I wanted to feel the serenity of his presence and to renew my commitment to the path that we felt far from back in Canada, my new home.

After our wedding in Cyprus, Ibrahim and I had travelled around India, Pakistan, and the Middle East, looking for and finding Sufi Sheikhs, but none of them had the charismatic presence of Sheikh Nazim. We still had not uncovered the mysterious process of purification which led to the mystical union, known as a "maqam" that was referred to in books about the Sufi path. I had witnessed the examples of Sheikh's wife, Hajja Amina, and that of Meryem. As far as I could tell, the practice for women seemed to be enormous service in whatever situation you were in and implementing the five pillars of Islam. Thus, you were following the outer and inner ways of Islamic Sufism.

Meryem had gone upstairs to take a much-needed rest after weeks of fasting and night prayers. Sheikh Nazim suddenly appeared in the kitchen. He was wearing a crumpled Turkish-style shirt and a simple prayer cap, which showed the grey stubble of his shaven head. Without his usual immaculate turban and overcoat, he looked more like an old village man and less like the idealized light-filled version in my heart. He looked around and barked, "Where is Meryem?" He appeared annoyed that she was not in her place in the kitchen preparing the food.

At once, I wanted to defend her. "She went upstairs to rest, Sheikh Nazim. She's exhausted."

Ignoring me, he turned around and went to the bottom of the stairs, yelling up, "MERY .. EM!" After waiting less than a minute, he stamped up the stairs to rouse her.

Soon, Meryem came down to the kitchen with red eyes, and she looked smaller than usual. She wouldn't look at me, and I knew she didn't want my sympathy or my sisterhood. "EstfirAllah," she said as she turned up the heat under the pot and stirred in the vegetables I had put next to it. I wondered where the compassion and respect that I had been told about as essential to Islam were at this point. I was hurt because she was upset and had been blamed for taking a much-needed respite from her burdensome duties. It was a struggle to try to explain this interaction and the disappointment felt at his perceived lack of appreciation for all the efforts that Meryem was making.

One explanation that justified Sheikh's actions came from another woman telling me, "The closer you are to him, the more he trains your ego, and the tougher he is on you. It is part of the Jihad al-nafs. It is a great blessing." Another explanation was that Meryem's nap meant that the food for the people at the mosque would be late or uncooked and this was behind Sheikhs concern. In a wider understanding though, I have always felt that my own bad inclinations and habits was something that I should have awareness and control over. In this philosophy, as in most mystical traditions, the disciple should regularly reflect on their thoughts, actions, and behaviours. Although an external authority should intervene if the disciple doesn't seem to be doing that, or if their individual behaviours have a negative impact on the group, then they can be gently corrected. It is not a question of a male or female authority calling out individuals, but a relationship of trust and spiritual guidance. Would that be what I would receive for my allegiance to Sheikh, or would I have to rely on Allah and Islam to give me appropriate spiritual guidance in this life or the next?

Sheikh Nazim's understanding of feminism was sadly limited to the belief that women were "envious" ones, and they were jealous of the freedom and opportunity that men had. This had been brought up in some conversations between Sheikh and his male followers, perhaps during consultations about "managing their wives," and it seemed to be implicit. It's not so strange that the only Sufi Muslim woman saint most people know of is Rabia al-Basra, who remained celibate and childless her whole life. Sheikh sometimes talked about his mother and clearly revered her. I never heard him mention his father, though. He told us his mother was a Mevlevi, which is the tariquat of Jalaluddin Rumi and the whirling dervishes, and he clearly saw his mother as the model for the ideal Muslim woman. The difficulty with this was that it meant that he did not place a priority on secular education, and the small amount of Qur'anic and Islamic education for many women was more "artisanal" than formal. Following tradition, Sheikh Nazim assumed that his daughters would get married and produce babies. Grand Sheikh Abdullah, the Sheikh of Sheikh Nazim, married his older daughter to her husband when she was fifteen.

A Visit to New Mexico:
Dar al Islam

੭৬

The Place of Islam, literally translated to Dar al Islam, was the paramount Sufi Muslim community of the mid-1980s. The second Christmas in Montreal, with three-month-old Adilia, we set off to visit the community and meet some of the senior mureeds of Sheikh who had encountered him and Grand Sheikh Abdullah Daghestani in the seventies. They had been part of the hippy migration and had found their spiritual goal in the tariquat.

Our journey started at the Michigan home of Abdul Hamid. I was surprised by his humble accommodation, which was a trailer in a park. This was very unusual for the son of a good Jewish family but, like Ibrahim, he had rejected the materialism of North America for a more meaningful life. The home had little insulation against the winter, but there was a wood stove and a warm welcome. His wife, Ruqiyah, was very kind and gentle and worked long hours at an office job to support them and their daughter. Abdul Hamid drove a delivery truck, but money was tight, and they lived very simply.

Abdul Hamid explained that his lifestyle was a conscious decision because it was the best way to support the full sunnah practices, the five prayers, and Jummah on Fridays. As well, the "distinctive uniform" of the turban and pants were a barrier to a more conventional better paying job. The walls of the trailer were thin, and I remember that Adilia kept everyone up most of the night, crying. My breast feeding had got off to a rocky start and although average length, Adilia was under-weight. I had continued to feed on demand but had not yet introduced solid food. I was still very much on the learning curve of being a new mother.

Ibrahim and I were hoping to get some insights into how the tariquat had adapted and evolved in North America in a very different society from either Damascus or sleepy Lefke. Abdul Hamid was astonishingly loyal to his Sheikh and the traditional model. He had introduced this version of Islam to other Muslims and non-Muslims, some of whom had converted and become mureeds through him. He had washed bodies and conducted marriages, repeating the instructions he received over the phone from Sheikh.

He had discovered that the most welcoming community was the Nation of Islam, Malcolm X Mosque, although when I visited, I found it a little awkward on both sides. In Montreal, we had connected with Tablighi Jamaat, which had several converts among it with whom I had become friends. Both groups had evolved independently of Saudi funding and educational programs. To most of the Muslim immigrants, though, we stayed an anomaly.

A few days later, we arrived in Albuquerque, New Mexico; rented a car and drove out into the desert. It was my first experience of the southern US, and I loved it. It seemed a suitable setting for an Islamic community, set up in the seventies with buildings designed by the world-famous Egyptian architect Hassan Fathy.

We arrived at a small and beautiful adobe home of a couple who were old friends of Ibrahim and were living in the community. As the lady was about to give birth to her fifth child, it was a difficult time for her to host. She was very relieved that for her birth, she was able to have a hospital stay and an obstetrician because of family connections. The other women used Mexican midwives they brought from over the border at night to deliver their babies, and they tried to align the births with the visits. Our hostess was very gracious, arranging a different dhikr of the Jerusalem Sufis. In addition, she gave me a pearl of hard-won wisdom.

"Look, women have always been oppressed, and in many Muslim countries, they still are. Just remember that in the first community, Medinah, they weren't. They had status. They had jobs. They had independent wealth. There are many women around now who have that also. We just don't get to hear about them."

From there, we went to stay with another couple who had a blended family and lived away from the community in a large adobe house that they rented. For them, owning their own house and some land was out of the question. They had a large family, which needed full-time care, and the children were home-schooled because of the lack of quality schools in the area. I didn't see much schooling taking place while I was there, though, perhaps due to a lack of books and other stimulation. In my teacher training, we always relied on resources either in the school or in the community, and this part was absent. The children were also isolated from their peers, which was their parents' choice because of criminal activity in the area. I felt this was very sad, and I wouldn't have wanted this for my own children.

As we moved around the area, meeting people, it was increasingly difficult for baby Adilia to settle. I worried that she was getting an ear infection from the frequent fluctuations in temperature and exposure to many other children, as I hadn't taken her many places before. I began to understand that babies are like plants and to get themselves off to a good start, it really helps if they have a stable home and a community.

A big realization came when we visited a family of ten children. They were attending public school as they lived in a house in a relatively good urban area. The children themselves were very well behaved and cared for, but I was shocked that one of the consistencies of the Naqshbandi mureeds was that they had huge families. The evening meal was like a school cafeteria with the smiling mother standing at the stove, ladling out bowls of pasta stew to the children around her. Some of them she called by name, but not all, and the girls took several bowls so that they could sit with younger siblings and help them to eat. The mother cared directly for the two youngest when she could. They also had another mureed who came in and helped some of the boys with their schoolwork because the parents didn't have the time to do it themselves. Sheikh Nazim had four children, but he had expressed a desire that he would have liked to have more. He saw them as a blessing from Allah.

On a Thursday, the evening of a Naqshbandi Dhikr, I was upstairs on one of the beds, struggling to get an increasingly upset Adilia to settle. The mother came in to offer some advice.

"You should give her a bottle. You just don't have enough milk. I never had enough. I was too tired, so I gave them all bottles, and I made a formula from a recipe they used at The Farm with Ina May Gaskin. If I were you, I would get used to it because Sheikh will want you to have a lot more!"

There in New Mexico, meeting these other older, more experienced women, I was forced to come to terms with my role as wife and mother. The reality that from the birth of my baby, my life was no longer my own, became clear. This was difficult to reconcile with the way I had always viewed my free-spirited life, although I had seen enough of the haphazard child-raising in other groups back in Lancaster to know that as a family, we would all benefit and grow from responsibility and stability. My priority was now to raise my child and manage my home. I desperately hoped I could find childcare and get some domestic help. I tried to accept the reality that "Dervish trips," wandering around exotic places, were no longer possible.

On our return to Montreal, the search for property and land outside of the city began in earnest. We were helped by Ibrahim's brother, Jeff, who was taking an interest in real estate and was an enthusiastic supporter of the idea of the Sufi commune. Every weekend, we would go off in the Honda Civic we had and visit properties and land within two to three hours' distance from Montreal. The Laurentians, the Eastern Townships, Estrie, and Western Quebec toward Ottawa.

When Ibrahim had told Sheikh Nazim about the project of Dar al Islam in the States, he had nodded and smiled and said, "Dar al Islam? Where is this Dar al Islam? Islam is everywhere! This is a good idea, but not a great one."

We didn't pay attention to the nuance in his speech. Like the mosque-building first-generation immigrants in Toronto, we did not consider the implications of long-term sustainability and that any commune or collective may work for a while but will eventually fail unless it is receiving constant renewal from the larger society around it.

After many months and what seemed like an endless number of properties, we arrived unexpectedly one evening in a small village near the Quebec border with the United States. We could just see Jay Peak at sunset, and the trees were large and healthy. It was Mansonville, Quebec. Ibrahim was very enthusiastic. I imagined the benefits of a rural lifestyle, and I loved the glorious nature. We searched for properties and eventually found a small four-season chalet with some land around it. The plan was that some of our fellow Naqshbandi would buy the land and build houses on it to have a small Sufi village. The reality, which we only realized after we had bought the property, was that none of them wanted to leave the city, and the only ones who did were planning to move to Ontario, threatened by the predominant French in the province. However, we were determined to try to fulfill the task that Sheikh Nazim had given us.

Sugarloaf Pond

❧

"All the way to Heaven is Heaven." Catherine of Sienna

L ike many bad decisions, buying the house at Sugarloaf Pond was a rational compromise rather than an enthusiastic action. It seemed as if we had exhausted our search, and this was the reasonable place to set up our Naqshbandi community. Weekends spent driving along back roads, looking at the mostly abandoned homes resulting from the drift of rural life to the city for families and small farmers, had worn us down. Eventually, this property was found that met all the criteria. In the Townships, winterized, and with land nearby for sale, which the other community members could buy to build their own homes. Although compact, it had four bedrooms and two bathrooms. There was a need for psychiatrists in the area, so Ibrahim could still work while we got the fruit and sheep business going. We bought it, but not the large parcel of land around it.

One weekend, we went down to the property from Montreal, where we were still staying during the week. It was a Friday afternoon, after Jummah prayer. Everything was ready for our trip ahead of time. Bags of clean clothes for every-one—Ibrahim, our thirty-month-old child, Adilia, and the baby, Amina, who was about six weeks old. As usual, I loaded up the Jeep with supplies, grocery bags full of food for the weekend, bags of diapers, and baby wipes. I also brought plenty of books and magazines, copies of *Harrowsmith* and the philosophical musings of Wendell Berry, of whom I was a huge fan. I didn't have much time to read, and the moments of respite from all the demands of daily living were always precious.

We hadn't been for a while. I had been exhausted from the birth and the difficulties of managing two young children, and I suffered from overwhelming fatigue in addition to mysterious joint swelling and back pain. It was the beginning of fibromyalgia, but I didn't know it at the time.

I told myself that once in the country, we could finally get the project of the Sufi community off the ground. I imagined that in a happy community of other young mothers and strong, willing men, everything would go well. We would work, celebrate and pray together and live from the abundance of our produce.

The chalet looked lovely in the autumn light when we arrived close to sunset. The trees in the encroaching forest had lost all signs of green, and strong winds had already blown away some of the gold and red leaves onto the ground around the long grass. A large pile of cut logs, which we had ordered, had been dumped in the parking space close to the door. Amongst other tasks, it was important that we split and stack them in a pile that we could access to feed to the wood stove that we had installed in the centre of the small living room. This warmed the house far more efficiently than the baseboard heaters we had to leave on to prevent the pipes freezing.

As we clambered out of the car and I released the babies from their car seats, waking them to their wails from sleep, the wind got stronger and decidedly colder and tiny flecks of ice dotted my down coat and scarf.

We went in, Ibrahim lit the stove to get a fire going, and I put a large pot of water to boil to make some spaghetti, an easy and quick meal for supper. We always avoided the fast food and greasy snack bars on the way because we were trying to eat as healthily as possible with the barakat of home cooked food. Although I have never noticed people eating spaghetti in Turkey, I told myself it was a reasonable compromise, as Italy was quite close and a Mediterranean country. Sheikh Nazim and his family never ate in restaurants or fast-food places, so as in many ways, we did our best to follow the pattern which we learned through their example.

After a quick supper, I settled Adilia down on the mattress in the small second bedroom on the ground floor. It was warm but bare. We didn't buy any furniture because there was no need. We were mostly living out of suitcases because of our frequent two-and-a-half-hour commute between a rented four-and-a-half in

Montreal and this, which we referred to as our home. After her long nap in the car, Adilia didn't want to sleep. Maybe it was the snow falling thickly outside that was exciting her. I have heard that the negative ions can influence children a lot. I read to her from the limited library that we kept there. Her favourite was *See How they Grow, Duck*, which featured lovely photos of a baby duckling as it comes out of the egg and then grows up to be a beautiful, proud, fully grown duck. In the last photo, it is standing in a child's plastic wading pool. That was the picture she liked best. In fact, her stated goal at that point when she grew up was "to be a duck." Unfortunately, at this point, we had not had time to fill wading pools and enjoy the summer. We had been too busy with renovations and commuting to do much else. I diapered and nursed the baby and settled her into a playpen close to the wood stove in the living room. She settled quickly into the warmth and quiet.

During the peaceful window of time that followed, I was able to pick up *Harrowsmith* magazine and immersed myself in an article about building a chicken coop out of wooden pallets. I needed to get my hands on some of those. That and railway ties were clearly a big part of the back to the country dream. What breed of chicken would I get? How many? Did I want them for meat as well as eggs? I noticed a strange mauve glow on the thick layer of snow now on the deck. It was then that the lights went out.

There was still some moonlight reflecting on the snow and cuddling baby Amina, I found my way to bed, which Ibrahim was already in, the covers curled tightly around his sleeping body.

I always had the same dark dream at the chalet, which I never understood. I was running through the woods being chased by a dark figure. Then I would find myself attacked and wounded. When I looked at my body with the bruises and gashes, it was not mine but a stranger. A woman with long, thin arms and tanned legs. On her slender ankle, she wore a gold ankle bracelet. These dreams, and the terror of assault and rape, were recurrent only when I slept at the house. Years later, we would discover that the previous owners we had bought it from were a couple from Switzerland, and they had left because the woman had a "nervous breakdown." After that, they were never heard from again, and the man returned only to put the house on the market. It was also significant that other women friends of mine who stayed at the house also had similar dreams. Perhaps that was why no other families had wanted to be part of this rural idyll so far. It was also a reality that none of them had the money to buy land or even a trailer to park on it. The mortgage we had was assumed by Ibrahim with the hope that, over the years, we could gradually build on this base.

I woke up early because the baby was crying in the crib next to me. As I nursed and comforted her, I looked out of the bedroom window in the grey light at the falling gobs of snow. I checked the light switch, and it was still dead, which was not the end of everything because the house was still cozy and it was daylight. These things were to be expected, and we also had brief power failures in Montreal. When I went to the sink to wash my hands, though, I was surprised because, after a brief trickle, no water was coming out. Had the pipes frozen again? We called our neighbour down the road. Fortunately, the Bell lines had not gone down, and he patiently explained that it was not the pipes but the water pump from the well, which was electrically operated. No, we did not have a backup generator. When I heard the toilet flush, I realized we now had a bigger problem than the unwashed tomato saucepan from the night before.

As we were processing this new reality, the phone rang. "Good, I got you," said Ibrahim's mother, now known as Bubby. "You'd better get back to Montreal! This snowstorm is going to be a biggy. Early for the year!" As always, Bubby's practicality weighed the balance and guided us. We would pack up our stuff and head back to the city. We could not stack the logs, clean the gutters, or do the autumn chores we had envisioned. For the city dwellers we were, safety was found in numbers and supermarkets.

As I packed up, Ibrahim swam through drifts to get to the Jeep, which now seemed far away across a white sea, and we could only make out the roof and the top of the windshield. He had grown up in Parc Extension, where the challenge was more digging your car out after the plows had passed. Armed with a new shovel he dug his way to the door. It was a relief to hear the Jeep start, but panic rose in my throat as the engine screamed and snarled as it tried to push its way out from the huge drifts. After what seemed like a long, long time, we both realized that even if we managed to get it out of the parking area, we would not be able to get it down to the lane to the unpaved road, which led to the start of the narrow tarmac byways, which led to the autoroute.

After some time reflecting on this new reality, I grabbed the spaghetti pot and went outside to fill it with snow. We would have water! After all, it was abundantly available in Allah's providence. We would survive. I remembered the stories I read of the first settlers, the "filles de roi,"[7] coming out to the tiny log cabins and surviving on beans, bacon, and wood stoves. I was proud of this adaptation, not yet mentioned in *Harrowsmith* articles. Maybe I would write one.

Another phone call to our kind and patient neighbour.

"Well, when the snow stops, they'll get out on the tractors. Brian's our guy. If you call him, I'm sure he'll put you on the list, being as it's an emergency like you said."

For the next forty-eight hours (about two days), we waited and hoped and prayed that the snow would stop. I boiled more spaghetti on the wood stove, which my little daughter ate with butter and cheese, but that we, the adults, only pecked at because we had lost our appetites. The toilet was starting to smell from not being flushed enough; it was like an airplane in there. I decided that because the snow was unfiltered, we should only drink it sparingly and only what we had boiled for five minutes. This also helped to reduce the trips to the toilet.

On Monday, the third day, while Ibrahim was busy phoning patients and cancelling appointments, the sun came out. The snow had stopped.

Brian's girlfriend listened compassionately to my pleas and promised that he would "get out to yer" as soon as it was possible. It was unexpectedly early this year, she repeated and then suggested that it would probably melt if we wanted to "hang on" for the rest of the week. She reassured me that this was only the situation a couple of times a year, more so in the winter. Farms were the priority, though. The lanes needed to be cleared to get the milk out and the mail delivered. The life of working people in the country obviously took precedence over the overwrought needs of those "from away."

I now had lots of time to read Wendell Berry and *Harrowsmith*, but I didn't have the patience for it. A narrative of wilderness survival would have been more appropriate because that was the one that was happening. Surviving in Canada is very different from life in a Mediterranean village. For one thing, in Turkey, it is possible to be outside for long periods all year round. For another, many fruit trees would freeze and die in this harsh climate. Animals would need to be kept warm, watered, and fed despite the temperatures. A chicken coop would need to

---

7   Wikipedia, s.v. "King's Daughters," last edited October 23, 2024, at 07:40 (UTC). https://en.wikipedia.org/wiki/King%27s_Daughters.

be very well insulated or inside a barn. Delicate people would perish, and in past times, I probably would have been one of them.

Exhausted from the weight of the snow pots carried in and the diapers and garbage out (to the Jeep, we couldn't leave them outside because of animals), constant shovelling, digging out from the wood pile at this point, feeding the wood stove, I knew that this was closer to a climactic punishment than a bucolic ideal. I remembered my great aunt, who lived on a homestead in Saskatchewan, saying, "Hell isn't full of heat. It's bitterly cold." The only duah I could think of was, "Oh Allah, please get Brian here as soon as possible so that we can get out."

Eventually, Brian's valiant tractor was spotted by Adilia, who was posted at the window looking out at the landscape, maybe for signs of ducks. I got so excited waving my arms and jumping up and down that Brian, looking warily from the tractor cab, might have figured I had "gone crazy." I remembered stories of survivors on desert islands spotting rescue boats or travellers in the desert seeing the palm trees of an oasis. Ibrahim grumpily suggested that I needed to "calm down."

I burst into tears once we were able to slide the Jeep down the narrow passage made for us and begin our gruelling journey back to what I now thought of as "civilization." Even baby Amina, sensing our relief, was smiling in the car seat beneath her woolly hat and snowsuit hood.

"Monchewhaal!" cried Adilia with delight when she saw the glass towers of downtown from the Champlain Bridge. سبحانه وتعالى وشكرا لله "Thank you to Allah Almighty," I repeated as I fingered the beads on my tesbih.

Now that I had realized the reality of the Quebec winter, I became a lot more interested in staying in the city. Although we had invested a lot of time and significant money in the project, it was only when the land around us was bought up by a developer who wanted to build "holiday chalets" that it became completely clear to Ibrahim and everyone else that this fruit tree community wasn't workable. It had been clear to Bubby all along. She was born in the Plateau and avoided the "country" as much as possible because it was dull and she didn't like "roughing it."

After it had been on the market for a long time, the property was bought cheaply by a wealthy professional couple who rented it out to skiers in the winter and holidaying families in the summer. They only visited occasionally and paid locals to make neat woodpiles for them.

The Inner Sheikh

γ

A s my geographical and emotional connection with Sheikh became more distant, I came to rely on my own internal guidance system. We were a long way from London and Cyprus, and as his popularity was increasing, there were many more people who wanted his time and attention. At first, we could contact him by ringing Cyprus and going through various international exchanges to reach the Lefke. Sometimes, we would get through but often the call would go unanswered. Other times, mureeds who lived locally would answer the phone and agree to take a message or a question. This person would then go and ask Sheikh for an answer and in a second call after a day or two and we would find out what it was. In the past, this was also done through letters, but that had become difficult as the mail system in Cyprus was very slow. This process became more complex when Sheikh was travelling frequently, and it became difficult to reach anyone. Then Zachra who had set up a home next door to the tekke, was taking the calls and providing answers, but sometimes she would give her own opinion. Answers allegedly given by Sheikh would be cryptic or vague and didn't help to clarify at all.

Frustrated with this situation but following the Sufi directive to "always consult the sheikh" before taking a course of action, we were left to develop our own ways of getting answers. Where was our "Sheikh" at this point?

I began to rely more strongly on my dreams and the feelings and instincts I registered about people and situations. We can so easily get caught up in the appearance and narrative of what is happening, and that may be different from what is occurring. When we lose touch with what is important, other forces will come in to fill "the vacuum." What is happening "below the surface" may be much more significant than what we see or how we interpret the events that we react to at the time.

I had an initial bond of love and connection with Sheikh's family, and this helped me to establish and build my own family and lay the foundations for a life in Canada. Above everything, I valued laying strong emotional attachments and connections, which helped my resilience in difficult circumstances. Early childhood psychology has also described the importance of this process of attachment in human development and I had developed a strong bond with the people I had met in Cyprus when I first went there.

The emotional bonding process of the traditional relationship with a Sufi sheikh also reflects the natural process of attachment. Some texts address the deficits and difficulties within them, but unfortunately, this is always cast as a problem with the mureed rather than a difficulty with the sheikh or guru. Modern psychology cannot be ignored simply because a tradition is ancient and established. In the late eighties, some Western followers of Eastern traditions started to articulate the abuse or exploitation that they had experienced at the feet of their spiritual teacher. This is also a problem in communities of Christian contemplatives and other closed social systems. None of the mureeds that I knew experienced anything like that during this period; rather, the problem was that although we were supposed to be following Sheikh, if we couldn't contact him, then we couldn't follow him.

When we sit with others who have gone through similar experiences or when we meet someone who crystallizes values and goals that we aspire to, then, if it is possible, we try to form a connection with that person. Then, we internalize them within us. At times, we may hear them speaking quite clearly, for example, when they appear to us in dreams. Sometimes, these figures are so mixed with our own needs and desires that they bear little similarity to the truth of the original person, a psychological process known as "projection." In other cases, the "telephone" line becomes quite clear. This is when there is an alignment on a deeper level. When we "internalize" a Sheikh, we receive an imprint and, in every individual, this may be subtly different.

The process of discovering the Inner Sheikh, connecting to the hidden spiritual reality that the figure represents, lies in the balance between our love for our Sheikh, our purity of intention and our ability to put aside our own egos.

At the time of Prophet Muhammed (PBUH), many people witnessed and heard him speak and act in a wide variety of different situations and affairs. Later, these accounts were collected and became the body of the corpus of the Hadith. However, there are often many different nuances and accounts of the same situation. Consequently, what has been called a "science" (namely, the scholarly discipline of hadith criticism) was developed to codify the reliability and credibility of the various accounts.

* Gibril Fouad Haddad's translation of Mulla 'Ai al-Qari, Encyclopedia of Hadith Forgeries (2014).

❖ ❖ ❖

Fana Fi Sheikh

In our eagerness to 'merge our inner selves' with that spiritual essence of a sheikh we may end up replicating the very same errors and omissions that our spiritual and religious teachers have as human beings. Worse, we may refuse to acknowledge that the compromises and weaknesses of human beings have created some difficult and morally dubious situations.

A frequent mistake in mureeds is to follow the example and the lessons of a sheikh blindly, ignoring the differences in life situations, personality, temperaments and circumstances. A very "soft-hearted" mureed will internalize much of the love and compassion of their Sheikh, while a greedy and manipulative one may well take examples of actions and justify them for his own uses and purposes.

Another pitfall is the cognitive dissonance, the gap between the interior model of the Sheikh and our own specific situation. How do we follow an Ottoman model in twentieth-century North America?

The early Muslim community shared many resources with each other, and prominent figures gave or loaned money to finance defensive armies and essential equipment, as well as providing food, clothing, and housing for the destitute. The community around the Prophet Muhammed (PBUH) in Medina forbade the use of exploitative interest on the part of the lender. When loans were given, they were without interest; the blessing of the loan was enough. It was very important that the tribe of the borrower pay back these loans in the case of death or further destitution, unless the lender forgave them.

Early Muslims operated on a cash or trade economy and, as a result, many Muslim rulings of Islamic law (Sharia) forbid the use of loans based on interest. The modern banking system rests on the interest generated by loans, however, and modern economic development is built on them. When people participate in it, then they are immediately enmeshed in the whole issue of credit cards and mortgages and car loans. It is nearly impossible to pay cash for many of our needs in Western society. This was one example where there was a disconnect between "traditional life" and the life of those in the West. The mureeds who inherited family money or businesses did well, but those who did not have those resources struggled.

Sheikh Nazim would recommend marriages between people who hardly knew one another or counsel people to set up businesses that had little chance of being successful. This happened repeatedly and witnessing it over the years led us to being disillusioned with some of the answers given by him. Ironically, one of the youngest generations of family members once confided in me, "Well, you know he is a very wise man, but he has some outdated ideas . . ." There were other "blind spots," such as the Turkish cultural bias and seeing psychological problems and mental illness as indications of a lack of faith that might be cured by spiritual interventions.

One example, Ibrahim was constantly told to "stop practising psychiatry." As the eldest son in a Jewish family, he had gone to medical school at age sixteen, not fully realizing the lifelong commitment he was making to healing the sick. He had to spend all day listening to and trying to help people with intense suffering and anguish, many of whom had lost all meaning and significance in their lives. Multiple levels of failure in our society, inadequate medical care, economic injustice, and little social support were very clear in his office patients. The only tools he was allowed by his professional corporation were pharmaceuticals, psychological interpretations, and referrals to other professionals. Any professional who deals with suffering will eventually start to feel the psychic burden of doing it, and perhaps Sheikh Nazim knew that this was what was troubling him. Also important though was that we needed him to "earn a living" to support the growing family. The irony was that on one side, Sheikh Nazim was urging me to "have more children" and at the same time urging Ibrahim to quit the job that provided for me and those children.

If I was going to have more children, we needed a stable housing situation. If we did not get a mortgage, then we could not afford a home and would have to pay rent on unmaintained housing. In addition, Sheikh Nazim believed that mothers should not work outside the home. The reality of the need for a two-income household was not clear to him.

Another issue was education. His own children had limited schooling, although some attended madrassas in Istanbul. In the tariquat at that time the emphasis was entirely on knowing the essential details of Islamic practice and a few suras from the Qu'ran. The next generation of Sheikh Nazim's grandchildren, however, were sent to expensive private schools and universities. Later representatives of the Sheikh would claim authorship of credentials and qualifications, which they didn't have, to give themselves status. They were especially aware of the social status connected to academic qualifications, such as medicine or engineering, within the Muslim community.

There is a lack of respect given to pious people who studied at madrassas or traditional institutions of learning, in contrast. The choice of sending children to train in technical subjects that led to high incomes was an indication of the values and social direction of those representatives. These were not the values of Sheikh himself, who had left an engineering degree course to study Sufism when he was a young man.

A spinning top, unless perfectly balanced with the forces around it, inevitably goes out of control. The top must be equally balanced, and the weight distributed down from the central pole. As long as the top is spinning on its axis, its direct centre of gravity, then it stays stable and balanced. When it loses its centre of gravity, the top spins in the heaviest direction. The flaws in the top mean that the heaviest part will always lead to the failure of the enterprise. It was the same with our tariquat. It lost its centre of gravity as the pull of the heaviest part went toward the earth.

We had reached another impasse on our spiritual life journey. We observed the five pillars of Islam, but the well of inspiration was dry without the generator of our beloved Sheikh. He was travelling more and more, staying in now-established communities throughout Europe and beyond. Lefke was filling up with residents and devotees, and it was becoming increasingly impossible to reach him. Although we still had a deep connection in our hearts with the Sheikh Nazim we knew, it was gradually growing weaker, and our inner guidance system, our 'Inner Sheikh', was becoming more reliant on the traditional Islamic sources that we were learning, such as Quran and hadith.

I decided that what we needed to do was set up a "women's circle" to get together and do dhikr and other spiritual practices to support each other.

What is Dhikr?

❧

"What is a dhikr?" my friend asked me.

"That's what we call our gathering . . . We recite the names of Allah and make duah. It's like meditation, you know."

The problem was that she didn't know. "Meditation? What's that?"

From my academic background in comparative religion, I had experienced collective sitting meditation, as well as chanting and singing. There was also the ecstatic dancing with the Michael energy groups. I had visited Buddhist monasteries and Hindu shrines over the years.

The first time I attended the Naqshbandi Dhikr in an old church in Cyprus, I tried to keep my back straight and chin up. The women sat together slightly away from the men in the part of the mosque that was reserved for them. I noticed an older woman had her nylon-covered legs stretched out in front and had put her coat over them. The ladies generally made sure that their feet faced away from the Qibla, the direction of Mecca, out of respect, but that seemed to be all. Being relatively comfortable on a hard but carpeted floor took precedence over most things because the dhikr usually went on for over an hour. The mosque was cold and dark.

Sheikh Nazim was loudly repeating some phrases—"Ya Allah"—and the other men were mumbling along slightly behind. It wasn't very musical, and Sheikh Nazim sounded strained. One of the men had a deep bass voice, which was pleasant, but there wasn't much effort to keep the voices together or to create any kind of harmony, so it wasn't choral. Also, it didn't appear to be very contemplative. Nobody had their eyes closed or appeared to be immersed in an altered state of consciousness. No one seemed to be in any sort of 'Hal' (spiritual state often elevated) or even putting out much effort to get one, except maybe me. I just got the feeling that Sheikh Nazim was pushing out the words like a kind of pneumatic drill, trying to break through thick cement . . . "Haqq. Haqq. Haqq." At one point, when I opened my eyes, I saw one of the teenage boys checking out the ladies.

It was a little underwhelming, even disappointing to me. I wasn't getting any kind of ecstatic hit, and that was what I wanted. I had wrongly assumed that initiation into the tariquat and participation in the practices was the golden ticket to Fana fi Allah (a mystical state of union with Allah). Once again, I was back down on the ground with my feet pinned to the floor. What was this Naqshbandi Dhikr at the heart of our tariquat? The ritual that I attended and the form of it that we subsequently practised in Montreal were the result of a long line of transmission, which Sheikh Nazim had received in Damascus from Grand Sheikh Abdullah Dagestani. I do not know how much these specific practices had been modified or altered when they finally came down to us.

Dhikr (literally, invoking, recalling, remembering) is a form of prayer assigned by a Sheikh and can have a collective and an individual form, can be either silent or vocal and involving movements. It consists of rhythmic repetition of the names of God and suras from the Quran in a specific format that is unchangeable because it is said to have a specific numeric value. What is being invoked, recalled, and remembered? The answer to that depends on who you ask. Deep states of mystical consciousness and personal revelation can accompany the practice, and, often, there is a palpable sense of peace and presence at the end of the ritual. On a mystical level, every part of the creation is said to be in some form of dhikr, even stones. For people, it is an essential practice to align the heart with the divine and free the nafs from its engagement with worldly and selfish desires. How effective the group dhikr often depends on the intentions and spiritual level of the people who are participating in and leading it.

In addition to the Naqshbandi group dhikr every Thursday, there was also a personal one. I was given a typewritten sheet of this little-known practice, an individual daily dhikr called an Awrad, which could be done after any of the five daily prayers, but it was recommended that it be done regularly and with sincere intention. It was designed to cultivate a state of spiritual support and involved concentrating on and mentioning the attributes (names) of Allah. It also included parts of the weekly practice, as well as some individual duah and passages from the Quran. I enjoyed this individual practice and did it regularly to try to connect my heart and soul with the source, to give me hope and deepen my connection with the divine.

The weekly group dhikr that we hosted was a lot of work for me: cleaning, shopping for food, cooking, inviting people, and pressing invitations for dinner. I saw it as an important service to Sheikh and the wider Montreal community, and as part of the pledge we had made to try to extend the influence of Sufism and Islamic spirituality. I used to try to get conservative Muslims to attend by asking them to dinner and then springing the dhikr on them before the food. Our Sufi practices were still seen as "un-Islamic" by many Montreal Muslims. Sometimes, the women were so used to just sitting in the kitchen and talking that that was what they did. We wanted them to have experience of an inner spiritual life, which at that time, was in contradiction of the exoteric Wahhabi-influenced schools and institutions.

❖ ❖ ❖

Ladies Dhikr

I had been trying to clean most of the morning, working backwards from the 3:30 p.m. deadline.

Why 3:30? Well, socializing was supposed to take place between our morning work and the evening "husband and family" time. It couldn't be lunch-time, so it had to be after Dhuhr prayer and Siesta/nap for the children, and before Maghrib, when it got dark and we should close the curtains and pray, so Salat al Asr (the afternoon prayer) it was. My plan was that we would meet at my place, do the dhikr, pray Asr, have tea and then depart. It was a lot more complicated, however.

A converted Muslim, Ricksha, arrived at 3:29 exactly. I was in the bathroom doing my ablutions because I had just cleaned the toilet again after potty training and wanted to be sure.

"Oh," she said with disappointment when I showed her into my living room with a futon covered in a blanket, a kilim rug, and several IKEA bookshelves. She was looking horrified toward one corner.

"You have turtles! Is that permissible? I mean, isn't the water dirty? What if it splashes on the prayer area or . . ." she lowered her voice to a dramatic whisper ". . . one of them puts their hands in it?"

Right on cue, the fattest Ninja Turtle, Annie, jumped off her perch into the water with a plop. Ricksha's son, five-year-old Jabber, screamed and hid behind her.

"He doesn't like animals. He can't be near them. He's afraid!!"

"How about I put a cloth over them? Look, there's a lid over the tank, so the water can't get out." I hurriedly draped an extra headscarf over the offensive tank.

I hadn't even thought that my daughters' pets could be so dangerous.

The phone rang; a Caribbean lilt warmed my heart. It was another friend. "What's this about a tea party? You going to have cake?"

"Well, it's a dhikr, um, remembrance of Allah . . . and err, I do have ginger biscuits . . ."

"Hmmm . . . well okay then. Don't start until I get there."

Good, so now we have two adult guests and the children's room is starting to look like a daycare.

I was carefully laying out the prayer mats and Ricksha was verifying the direction with her pocket prayer compass when the phone rang again.

"You got the car? I need a lift from the metro. That bus route is lousy."

I pleaded with Ricksha, who had a nice new car, and she slowly put on her coat and that of Jabber and went to pick up another guest and her kids. As Ricksha was leaving temporarily, I saw Sammar making her way up the stairs. She had three rowdy boys in tow: Abdul Latif, Abdul Rahman, and another one. There seemed to be a fight breaking out.

"Salaams! I thought you only had two."

"Yeah, this is the cousin, Abdullah; he wanted to come for the party . . ."

Sammar collapsed on the futon and put her feet up. At six months pregnant, she was already tired.

There was some yelling from the kids' room after the boys entered, and then some screams. My eldest came running out, and a Barbie head flew over her like a hand grenade. A boy burst into the living room, holding the headless doll corpse in front of him. "Ack ack ack . . ."

"Oh, these kids," Sammar groans, "they are driving me nuts."

After herding, cajoling, bribing, and then, finally threatening—"This is serious . . . any more disturbances and I will turn off the video, and there will be no more *Little Mermaid*, got it?"—the children were contained in a bedroom, and we had the living room.

The ladies were sitting in a circle, and I handed out the photocopied sheets I had prepared, which had the text, translation, and transliteration of the Noble Naqshbandi Dhikr.

"I don't read Arabic!" someone said.

"The words are underneath; you just have to say them," I replied.

"Yeah, like I said, I don't read it. I only read French."

"Maybe you could just join in, then?" I pleaded.

"What do you mean 'join in'? I don't use those beads; they're haram. You must use your fingers to count EstfirAllah . . . otherwise, you won't be resurrected on Judgment Day with your hands full of Noor . . ." said another of the guests.

"Where did you get this?" Now, all the guests were objecting.

"Are you authorized? Only an Imam from Saudi is authorized to teach Quran and recite, my husband says, and he knows because he's from Pakistan."

"I'm not leading it . . . it's the repetition of the names of Allah . . . you know the ninety-nine names?

"Please?" was my last attempt to get this going.

After an uncomfortable pause and some more negotiation, "Perhaps we should just say Fatihah?"

"Only to ourselves . . .! We're not saying it in Jamaat; we're not authorized."

"I'm not praying Asr. I only pray at home."

Just then, the door was pushed open, and we saw the first smiling face. "Now, where's that cake you promised us?"

We had a tea party and a pleasant social exchange. My daughters had bruises, and some of the Lego was missing the next day, but it was fun. I never tried to repeat the event.

Potluck at the Local

❧

How come none of them are praying Sunna? I wondered, distracted from my prayers by the passing of feet in front of me and bodies bumping me from behind. A mass of large women draped in black surrounded the trestle table with the potluck Iftar on top. I pushed my way through toward the food. I have never been good in crowds, and I was a bit intimidated by the gregarious groups of women, none of whom I knew or who acknowledged me, a stranger. It was a good turnout, though, for the Muslim community, and it was hosted at a community centre by colleagues of Ibrahim.

I was looking for the large Pyrex dish of stuffed zucchini that I had brought, wrongly imagining that even if there was no rotisserie chicken or samosas left, then at least I would be able to eat what I had brought. When I spotted the dish at the end, it was empty, surrounded by other large empty pots and used plastic cutlery.

With the clean fork I found, I tried to scrape up some leftover, yellow-coloured rice and a few pieces of iceberg lettuce and onion onto a Styrofoam plate, all the time telling myself that this was very good training for my nafs. Whenever I met a challenging situation in the community, when I became overwhelmed with the difficulties of cultural cliques, other languages, or the struggle for survival that fostered a cloud of despair in many of the new immigrants to Quebec, I reminded myself to try to detach from the situation and make an internal dhikr. Sometimes, though, the voice in my head got loud and the dhikr would become

71

a kind of internal monologue of my needs and wants. Now triggered by hunger and sadness, the voice started to rise . . .

Oh Allah, please give me patience and compassion. Help me to support my sisters and bring the barakat of Ramadan and your blessing to us all. I still fondly remembered Taraweeh at Peckham.

The TV screen on the wall flashed on with an image of a hairy foot, but there was no sound . . . after a few minutes, the screen went black again, but then all our heads turned in rapt attention as the head of a handsome, dark-eyed young Asian man with a white Kofi began to chant . . . "BBBEEESSSSMilllah . . . bassem alleh al-rahman al-raheem, In the name of Allah, the most merciful and the most compassionate."

It was times like these that my faith and identity as a Muslim were sorely tested. After the initial euphoria and congratulations of being a newly married convert had worn off, I was left to negotiate the ways and means of very different cultures and understandings of our deen. The world of Islam is multi-faceted and global; subsequently, the behaviours, languages, and ethnicities of Muslims are widely different, united by the tenets of belief and the practices. I was a double foreigner, if you like. I had converted to Islam and then emigrated to another country. I had transitioned from swinging single girl to wife and mother in a very short space of time, as well. It wasn't surprising that I was a little lost. I had put on a scarf and covered my body. I had also put on a huge amount of weight, birthed babies, and nursed them a process which also radically changes your sense of identity.

Initially, my mother really didn't know what to make of this change. I seemed to be a completely different person from the daughter she had known previously. Her own spiritual journey had been to a convent in Kent, England run for ladies with substance abuse problems. Once there, my mother had thrived. It was rather like the boarding schools she had attended from an early age. With the support of a fierce Irish Catholic sister, she had maintained her sobriety and made peace with herself. It was almost miraculous and may also have been that before the intervention, Sheikh Nazim had made duah to Grand Sheikh Abdullah Daghestani. Whatever it was, we were both in a much better place, and we began to build a good relationship. She quite liked my Islamic born-again Muslim marriage, and she adored her grandchildren. Her daughter had become more domestic, more stable, and responsible. Her major discomfort, however, was . . . "that thing on your head," which was her way of referring to the headscarves I was wearing.

She seemed to have completely forgotten that up until a decade before, she and her friends all wore hats or scarves on their heads when they went out, and especially if they went to church. One of her friends asked me earnestly, "Does he make you wear that thing?" This might have been based on the widespread idea that all Muslim women are suppressed and controlled by their husbands, as opposed to other women. My mother and her friends didn't know the word for "that thing"—Hijab. My favourite scarf was a pink cotton one with tiny tassels on it, which Hajja Amina had given me. I wore it proudly.

My mother said, "You look like an immigrant with 'that thing' on your head."

I said, "Mum, in Canada, I am an immigrant, and I have the card to prove it."

"Well," she said defensively, "you're not one here," referring to my presence in England.

A few years later, she excitedly called me to tell me that Jemima Khan, a wealthy heiress and convert to Islam who at that time was married to Imran Khan, was "wearing one" and had converted also . . . her headscarf was Hermès, so that made it okay. During her multiple hospital visits over the years, most of the people taking care of her were Muslims, employed by the National Health Service. She always told them her daughter had become a Muslim, and she usually received very kind treatment.

Taraweeh at Peckham

❧

I remember Peckham Mosque, a huge Victorian gothic building with a small
kitchen at the back and a cement yard with a corrugated iron fence protecting it from vandals and squatters.

Inside were dark tiled washrooms, then a huge main area which had been the
body of the church, which was the original building. The floor was covered in a
patchwork of rugs. There was a balcony along the right side and a small room
up a steep flight of stairs where I had stayed that first Ramadan with Zachra
and others. Triangular tiles, in geometric patterns, were used throughout, as
was the style of neo-Gothic Victorian buildings. The decorative elements were
borrowed directly from the Orient. There was a beautiful round stained-glass
window, which was also a geometric pattern.

I only visited during Ramadan when I was in London over the years. Then
the mosque was alive with people. Many visitors from the US and Europe came
there and stayed for the month and others passed through -some only in the
evenings because they lived in the UK. It was an eclectic mix that reflected the
broad appeal of Sheikh's message and the spiritual thirst of that time in the
late eighties.

I didn't sleep over as the needs of my young children and the bedbugs and
other disturbances made it overwhelming. If a woman was pregnant or nursing,
Sheikh would recommend that they make up the fast later as "they are already
receiving a lot of blessings by supporting their growing babies and serving their

families." Although this was a relief, it also meant that I was not fully participating in the action, and I would trek across London to try to get some barakah.

One night at the mosque, standing in the line, there was a particular feeling in the atmosphere. It was one of those "magical" nights. Perhaps it was Lailat al Qadr -the special night of Ramadan when the Holy Quran is descending to earth.

Harmonious lines of energy connected my heart with those around me, the old Turkish woman on a chair next to me, the young German girl on the other side. It became like it was not just my heart but a Universal Heart that was opening like a flower in the light.

The mureeds were lining up and then forming a circle, going round and round singing Salawat on Prophet Muhammad, peace and blessings be upon him. It seemed as if in the process of this, angels were ascending and descending like in an old medieval map of the world. All of this was happening in a broken-down mosque in a small part of fragmented London. It was as if that place had become one of the centres of the world where the breath of Allah could enter and give us spirit. We could be more fully alive; our hearts could beat in turn with the cosmic life keeping the planet turning in space by the will of God.

Later, I needed to remind myself of experiences like this and I was hoping they would replicate themselves in Canada. I really wanted the other Muslims to know what it was like to be in a context charged and alive with the flow of blessings, and to have the veils of the heart lifted if only for a brief glimpse of beyond.

The Issue of Polygamy

fter we had been married for a few years, Ibrahim had come to me with some news that was troubling him. "I don't want you to take this the wrong way, and I don't want you going around telling everyone," he began. Then the secret came out.

A man close to Sheikh had accompanied him to a house in London recently. There, a young woman had got married to Sheikh. The husband of Hajja Amina now had a second wife. This marriage was secret because it would upset Hajja Amina too much if she found out; that was the rationale. In the Muslim world, many of the few polygamous marriages that take place are hidden because all that is required is a couple of trustworthy witnesses and an agreement. I reminded myself of the clause in my marriage contract about polygamy, in my initial rush of anxiety and shock, it was that Ibrahim could not take another wife unless he had my permission, which was unlikely. Sadly, from that point on, I did not see Sheikh Nazim as the shining, benevolent patriarch he had been previously. Perhaps I was just growing up; perhaps something was changing within the paradigm of the tariquat itself. Grand Sheikh Abdullah Daghestani predicted that one day, Sheikh Nazim would have a bride in London, which was another rumour that circulated among the mureeds. This marriage became a widely known secret after a while. It was clear that some of the closer mureeds knew and were upset about it, but I never brought it up directly because it was just one of those things you didn't discuss. This was a private, behind-closed-doors matter, and, in any case, what business was it of mine? The Prophet Muhammad had many wives, and although it is permitted in Islam, there is the condition that all the wives are treated equally, which makes it almost impossible in modern times.

I was sad when I heard that Meryem and Selim had been pushed out of their vital role with Sheikh Nazim. This happened after the time Sheikh Nazim had married this younger woman, so he was now staying with her group and no longer above the shop in Peckham. They were the people who had helped to bring me into the tariquat, and I loved and respected them. Another concern was my loyalty to Hajja Amina and her family; it was a very important part of my involvement with the tariquat and the Naqshbandi order. For Ibrahim and me, this was also difficult because it meant that we and the other North American mureeds didn't have access to him in the same way after that. The annual Ramadan trips to Peckham were no longer possible.

A Trip to Peckham

ع

It was 62 degrees in London with a soft breeze that blew in the grey air. I was wearing my ankle-length belted black raincoat with a blue sparkly headscarf. On one shoulder, I carried a red purse with a zipper against pickpockets, and on the other, a very large diaper bag. Strapped to my chest was a snuggly in which my younger baby, Amina, now over six months and getting heavy, was snoozing. I had a stroller in which my older daughter, Adilia, was sitting wearing a yellow plastic Mac with ducks on it. She was happy as usual and playing with some pieces of elastic and wooden beads.

It required quite a lot of strength for me to stand and even more to manoeuvre. As I saw the red double-decker bus turn the corner of Hammers Lane, Mill Hill, I braced myself for the next hurdles, getting up the steps, stroller first, then paying my fare as the bus lurched forward. It was a combination of balancing and pushing my way inside the bus to try to find somewhere stable to perch or sit until we got to the tube station, where I would get off to continue the next part of my journey. I was getting used to it, though. Somewhere inside my head I told myself, *All these struggles are okay because it is Ramadan and every effort is rewarded.*

I was pumped with the adrenalin from my mission. *The timing must be perfect.* I had calculated two hours and twenty minutes for the voyage from North to South London—two buses and two tube rides—and that was the quickest route to Peckham. This is where Hajji Selim's shop and the zenith of Sufi consciousness,

Sheikh Nazim, should be at that time. This was to be one of my last visits, but I was unaware of it. I had to catch Sheikh after Dhuhr nap, before Asr talk, and before departure to have an Iftar dinner somewhere where he would become inaccessible. That was the Ramadan schedule, and after several years' experience on my Ramadan trips to London, I knew it. It was so important to me that I connect with the inspiration and blessing that I always felt in his presence. The mureeds and people around him were often special and interesting also, and I enjoyed the interactions and meetings of hearts that happened frequently.

Sitting in the dark, dusty tube train with a few minutes' rest between stops, having snacked, suckled, and settled my babies, I tried to articulate my frustration with the domestic situation I had found myself in. How did this happen? I went with the flow and followed advice and guidance from my trusted Sheikh, and this was the result?

I am no longer the author of my own destiny. I have no career of my own. I cannot work in Quebec because the government doesn't think my qualifications are valid. The worst part, though, is that I feel like a drudge and a negative overweight whiner. I hate my life. I am too tired, fed up, and sick to jump out of bed most days, and yet I do, dragging myself around my untidy apartment, changing diapers, cooking food, and trying desperately to make my children's lives as good as possible. I adore them and am trying to give them as meaningful a childhood as I can. When their father comes home, he is the target of my hostility and pain. It is okay for him, I tell myself. He gets to control the resources, and his own schedule.

On our yearly visit to our spiritual well, Ibrahim was down there in Peckham, hanging out with the boys, laughing, joking, and basking in the glow of the Baraka flowing forth. I camped out with the children at my mother's flat—enormously preferable to the mosque in Peckham, with constant conflicts between those camping out there, and no hot water. Despite all the difficulties, he was close to Sheikh, and I was not. A message had been sent back to me that it is "better you stay with your mother," which was also convenient for mureeds because my young children might well be disruptive to the talks and events taking place. Sheikh was right but I still wanted them to have the benefits of interacting with him as I believed that he was a unique being that they were unlikely to meet anywhere else.

When I became a Sufi Muslim, I was told the simile of the precious jewel. It goes something like this. If you have a precious jewel, you do not leave it lying around, but you keep it in a velvet case with care in a safe place. A woman is like a jewel, and her husband should keep her in her lovely home where she has ease and comfort, and she can shine with divine light.

My not so lovely box was far away in francophone Montreal, the other side of a large ocean. It was an upper duplex, with a negligent geographically distant landlord who wouldn't fix anything, drafty windows and a toilet that blocked on a regular basis. We were all ill most of the winter because the temperature was controlled by the malevolent tenant downstairs, who was out all day and didn't want to pay for heating.

"You refused to stay in our home in the Eastern Townships," Ibrahim reminded me. "You chose to live here because it is near the mosque and a park for the children. You are never satisfied; you are always complaining, although you have so much more than so and so ..." often using the example with a recent immigrant woman who I have never met because she doesn't go out of her apartment. The reports of mythical exemplary Muslim wives and mothers are usually via their male relatives, and so I consider them unreliable. Raising young children is very difficult for both parents, and the situation was not helped by Sheikh Nazim telling his male followers that they should not be changing diapers or waking up at night to feed the children because it is "not their role." I can only make peace with this idea when I understand that this is part of an intergenerational context of relatives who raise the children and run the family businesses collectively. This was not the world I lived in. My mother tried to help—buying shortbread from Marks & Spencer to feed the children—but she could not manage my leaving them with her for more than a few minutes.

The biggest problem with the jewel comparison is that it is not my narrative. I wanted to be Freya Stark.[8] I wanted to ride out with a caravan of Bedouins and chart unknown geographical areas. I wanted to meet with mystical men and women and share our spiritual insights and secrets over campfires in ancient places. I wanted to live in the mystic East and rise before Fajr every day to drink in the ocean of mercy that is the love of Allah.

Although, I also wanted to be entertained, to read books, to laugh and shop and gossip and have an independent income with no one to tell me what to do.

---

8   Dame Freya Stark, British Italian explorer & travel writer, 1893-1993

Oh yes, and if dreams came true, I would also lose twenty pounds and have a full-time nanny and a housekeeper.

I didn't think Sheikh Nazim could help me with those last ones, but I knew that he had a miraculous knack for seeing what the problem was and then suggesting a workable solution.

Please, Allah, I pleaded inwardly, *please let him be there and let me talk to him.* Every time I went there were more and more people wanting a piece of him, like a celebrity. There was no longer the time for leisurely chats and mild jokes and time spent together like before. It was all different. The predetermined agenda was followed. Iftar meals were scheduled in advance at wealthy London homes. There were self-appointed drivers and assistants. Women and children were at the back of the crowd. I missed the old days and cherished the memory of my times in Cyprus with the Sheikh's family. He was out of reach and so now I had to strategize.

Not many of the mureeds knew there was a laneway behind Hajja Meryem's shop for deliveries and garbage pickup. This was the laneway that the white minivan came down to pick up the Sheikh and take him places. There was a wrought iron garden gate and a little patch of grass with a line of flagstones leading to a backdoor, which had been recently installed and had pink fibreglass stuffing poking out around the sides. Someone had not got around to finishing off the framing. There were a lot of things like that around the Turkish Cypriot infrastructure here in Peckham. The English mureeds thought it was a terrible problem because of safety and standard British rules, regulations and codes, which were ignored. On the other side, I found the flexibility and willingness to improvise refreshing.

The wheels of the buggy bumped and twisted along the uneven surface of the laneway, and just when I looked at the backs of the shops trying to figure out which one; a door opened. There he was. An emerald-green pointed hat with a stout white turban wrapped around it. The face under it full of light, a wise intelligent glance in the large blue eyes and a long white beard like a length of silk going down to his heart. He wore his ankle-length grey overcoat and, in his hand, reaching forward there was a walking stick.

Aha. The moment is here. My weariness fell away like a shadow at midday. I was under the light now, moving in grace, pushing the garden gate open with the stroller and efficiently blocking the exit. He was caught. They had to get past to get to the van, which was now coming up behind me. The driver glared at me as he stopped a few feet away.

Just behind Sheikh—they would rather be besides, but the doorway is narrow—were two of the London mureeds. They wore the uniform; black Damascus-style sherwal, a white collarless shirt, and green waistcoats. They also wore the obligatory white turbaned hats, but the wrap wasn't as large as that of Sheikh, "out of modesty." Besides, they were getting enough attention already. Their self-appointed role was to "shepherd" Sheikh Nazim, to keep him on schedule and to protect him from women like me who would bother him, just like I was planning to do.

Sheikh Nazim saw me, of course. He recognized me now that there was no one standing in front of me, blocking his vision. He smiled a little and raised his eyebrows very slightly. I looked directly into his eyes, and I laughed. It was a joy. This was the pot of gold at the end of the rainbow, which came after the storm. The clouds had cleared; both my children were awake now. They knew at once, with an uncanny instinct, in touch with their mother's body, something good was going to happen. The older one, at only just over three, knew that the Sheikh might well give her a sweet. Yes, coming closer, he reached into his pocket and pulled out two wrapped toffees. He gave one to Adilia and held one in front of the baby's face. Obviously, she was too young to eat sweets, although she pushed out her tongue, sensing food.

"Ah!" he said. "Good, Munirah, you may have it for her."

Sheikh Nazim had regulated many aspects of the birth and upbringing of these two. We asked for their names. He had told the mothers that a child had a right to nurse for two years. Bottle feeding was not approved. At this point, I had two girls, and I was exhausted. I have been described, amongst other things, by Sheikh as "a weak one." Every time I was pregnant, I was encouraged and cajoled to produce a boy. As if I had any control over it; scientific studies told me that I didn't, but Sheikh and many other Muslims thought I did, so it had become yet another issue in my marriage.

The procession out of the door had come to a halt. The engine of the van was running.

As I was pocketing the toffee to save for later, one of the bodyguards shoved his way in between me and my Sheikh, cooing, "Ya Effendi . . ." and trying to grab Sheikh's elbow to guide him around this obstacle and toward the van.

Sheikh smiled and pulled his elbow away. The mureed froze like a sheepdog. "Alhumdulillah," he said to me, "another baby is coming...?"

I didn't know if this was a question, a statement, or a prediction. My mind scrambled, wondering what this was about. *Is he talking about someone else?* As he was nodding his head and it seemed we were still in conversation, I seized the moment...

"Sheikh Nazim..." I began, "I am very tired. My husband is very tired..."

Sheepdog mureed grabbed Sheikh Nazim's elbow again now as I was speaking, and his colleague was pushing from behind. They were still trying to get him toward the van and away from this annoyance. This really was not the time to start talking about marital dissatisfaction, and worse, my statement was making Sheikh Nazim chuckle, and so the mureeds now began smiling and then laughing, "What a joke, no more babies. Her husband is too tired."

Now Sheikh Nazim would defend his mureed's honour at my perceived, misinterpreted slur. "Doctor Ibrahim is a strong man, mashallah. You must give him what he is asking!"

Now the mureeds were nodding and snickering and had managed to get him on the other side of me nearer to the van. A sliding door in the side had been pulled open for their sainted passenger.

My heart hit the gravel, prickling tears pooling in the corner of my eyes. I had journeyed this far and struggled this much, and this was what I got. *Ya Allah, in you only can I put my trust,* I said in my mind.

Before he got into the van, Sheikh Nazim turned around and looked at me and the children again. Perhaps he saw the effect of this interaction, or maybe this was just habit, but he stopped, stood still, and raised his hands in duah.

At this sign, everything else stopped, even it seemed, the clouds in the sky. Both mureeds and the van driver imitated his posture. He closed his eyes and was reciting something I couldn't hear, but I knew at the end of a duah he always said the Fatihah, so I said that also.

The duah lifted me away from disappointment, exhaustion, and frustration. My heart was once again in cool, clear water. Although the tears must run their course, and they would, I had hope that one day my heart would be at peace, and I would be aligned with my life. One day, it will not be as hard, and my life will not be so difficult. I felt light and certainty. *Allah is real.*

"Daddy!" exclaimed Adilia, and there he was. Ibrahim was walking behind the van.

"Salaam alaikum," he said.

"Wa alaikum as salaam . . ." I replied. He was with us again and had not gone off in the van.

He had come back to his family. Life at the mosque had become intolerable. People had been queuing up to get psychiatric advice, and it was exhausting. He couldn't get any peace. We headed back to my mother's, hoping we could get a nap before Iftar.

✧ ✧ ✧

The "problem" it was made clear, was not pregnancy but rather the gender of the babies I was producing. In traditional patriarchal societies, there was a high premium on male children, who could provide resources and cash for the family. In the Naqshbandi tariquat, the patriarchy was alive and well. Women had some authority in the domestic sphere and with the upbringing of their children, but their contributions were constantly discounted, and this became worse over time. I eventually had three daughters, and although some people expected me to "keep going until I had a boy," I always knew my daughters were an amazing gift that should be appreciated fully. In the society I lived in, girls had many more opportunities, and I wanted them to know them and flourish.

It was a habit in the tariquat to ask Sheikh for a name for the unborn child. Our first child was given the name Othman and became Adilia. Our second child was to be Shamsuddin and became Amina, and the third child was to be called Isaak and became Sara, although Sheikh Nazim had also suggested the name Leikha, which none of our Arab sources had ever heard of and which was the name of the first dog in space. I didn't want to name my child after a canine astronaut who had perished. I have only recently learned that there is a Turkish name La'ika, which means "worthy," but I chose the name Sara for my third child partly because I was fed up with Arabic names that nobody could pronounce, and Sara (Sora in Russian) was the name of Ibrahim's grandmother, a formidable Jewish matriarch who managed her own business, a general store on Park Avenue, for many years after emigrating from Russia to Canada.

The pressure to have a male child continued the entire time I was in the tariquat. It was used as a weapon against me by one of Sheikh's North American representatives later. Many years after Peckham, this representative was visiting and sat holding court in our living room in Ville St. Laurent. I was in the kitchen, preparing food for the guests and running an impromptu welcome centre by dispensing tea, coffee, and other requests—answering the phone, taking messages and so on. For some reason, at one point, he said in a dismissive way, "Inshallah Munirah will have a boy, and Ibrahim will not have to take another wife."

I quickly retorted, "Inshallah, I am making duah that you will have a girl so that you can appreciate the wonderful love and the fine qualities that they bring." I didn't have a son, Ibrahim did not take another wife, but this person had a daughter a little while later.

A Visit with Mrs. Tweedie

❧

We met at Willesden Green tube station—Ibrahim, another couple, and me—because we had heard about Mrs. Tweedie, a female Naqshbandi Sheikha living in England. We wanted to meet her. Many Western Sufi group members were wondering about the role of women in Sufism. Every Thursday afternoon, Mrs. Tweedie held what was referred to as a "gathering" where she lived. We were curious because she seemed to have integrated Western non-Islamic words and practices into her group. This was a great opportunity.

We walked along the maze of suburban streets in Willesden, London Borough of Brent, looking at the classic pebble dash and "pseudo-Tudor" semi-detached houses. Most of them had a peek at the roofline above the door, which was decorated with wooden rays in a sunrise pattern, and many also had the original front doors, with small stained-glass inserts in the top. These houses were more than quaint to me because, growing up in North London, many of my friends lived in these "semis," as they were known, and they were the setting of many experiences—squats, punk parties, and so on. It felt very ironic that once more, I was returning to this dystopia, and this time, it was to meet another incarnation of oriental esotericism. My personal demographic, as a child of the 60s, was shaped by the second generation falling out of the economic house-owning boom of the post-war generation. There was no way that any of my peers could afford to live in one of these houses.

I had now come full circle because of the famous and unique character of this Sufi Naqshbandi teacher. The bell rang as we pushed the button in the middle of the front door. When it opened, we glimpsed in the narrow hallway the figure of a tall woman wearing a cardigan, blouse, and tweed skirt. Her white hair was pulled back tightly into a bun, and she had a strong face with steely blue eyes. She reminded me of someone's grandmother, and she looked cross. As we filed in, I took her hand to kiss, but she snatched it away and then turned her back on us. She didn't want to be treated like a guru, which was how she reacted to this gesture, although it was merely one of respect toward another or older person. The guru refusal stance was rather disingenuous because with her group sitting on the floor of the living room and with herself at the front in an armchair, giving instructions, that was exactly what she was.

"I am not a guru! I only want to tell my story and the truth!" she said frequently.

However, that had not been easy. Her first book, *The Chasm of Fire: A Woman's Experience of Liberation Through the Teachings of a Sufi Master*,[9] which chronicled her student hood with her guru in India, was edited so severely that she felt "compelled" to revise it completely and had just published a new edition called *Daughter of Fire: A Diary of a Spiritual Training with a Sufi master*.[10] It was at least three times larger and had a large, glowing portrait of her on the front cover. It had just arrived back from the printers. I bought a copy, cash, right there on the spot because I was very excited to read and learn from her. I had read the first book cover to cover because, like many of us, I wanted to know how to be an enlightened guru and give discourses from an armchair.

Mrs. Tweedie didn't like Islam very much. This might have been because she had been part of British society when Orientalism and colonialism promoted the idea that it was a "backward religion" in contrast to White Christianity. When the subject was brought up by Ibrahim, she became reactive and eyed us warily. She declared that Islam was "not necessary" in its outward form and the "real work" was the inner work of Sufism, which was a direct contradiction of every-thing we knew about the Naqshbandi tariquat in Turkey and in India. We later found out that the Naqshbandi Silsila, the "Golden Sufis," had a Hindu branch in

---

9   Irina Tweedie, *The Chasm of Fire: A Woman's Experience of Liberation Through the Teachings of a Sufi Master* (Element Books, 1979).

10   Irina Tweedie, *Daughter of Fire: A Diary of a Spiritual Training with a Sufi Master* (The Golden Sufi Center, 1995).

India, and that was the particular branch her guru belonged to. That was why she thought Islam was superfluous to Sufism. In contrast, we saw Sufism as the life force of Islam and the observance of the five pillars as a support of any mystical state reached. I didn't get around to asking her if she thought that Hinduism was also superfluous to Sufism. I suspect she might have said that yes, it was. Perhaps that was why she rejected the "guru" title. She was trying, in her own way, to make the spiritual process more democratic and egalitarian. Her original point of contact with Sufism had been the Theosophical Society, a nineteen-century medium and esoteric movement that mostly followed their own personal revelation and which was also started by a Russian woman, Madame Blavatsky.

The founder of the Naqshbandi tariquat, Baha-ud-Din Naqshband Bukhari, fourteenth-century BCE, was very skilled at dream interpretation and was often consulted. The gift of interpreting dreams can be transmitted to mureeds, although the earliest transcripts and manuals of dream interpretation are limited to "spiritual" subjects because psychology as a modern science did not exist at that time. This becomes problematic when you are working in a modern context because our understanding of the human psyche has been shaped by the science of psychology and the psychoanalytic work of Sigmund Freud and Carl Jung. (Katz 1997).[11]

Mrs. Tweedie's main disciple was Llewellyn Vaughan-Lee, who came down from upstairs. It was reassuring to learn that he was working as a Jungian analyst because C.G. Jung was the only psychoanalyst who was concerned with the spiritual dimension of the human psyche. Some members of the group recounted their dreams, and then Mrs. Tweedie definitively pronounced the interpretation of the dreams. Mrs. Tweedie had been given the gift of dream interpretation by her Sheikh/Guru, and she was very clear about her authority in these matters.

One of the followers asked for an interpretation of a recent dream they'd had. She described it, and then there was a genteel discussion of the symbolic meaning of hippos interspersed with polite laughter. It wasn't quite psychoanalysis; it wasn't group therapy, and it wasn't Sufism as I knew it. It was a unique combination of each, but I personally found it somehow dissatisfying.

---

11 Jonathan G. Katz, "An Egyptian Sufi Interprets His Dreams: 'Abd al-Wahhâb al-Sha'râni 1493–1565," *Religion* 27, No. 1: 7–24 (1997).

We had an enjoyable and cordial meeting, though. It was a pleasant change to be in an environment that was very "English." She liked babies, especially small boys, and she called up a young mother to sit next to her so that we could all gaze at the "living archetype of the Madonna and child."

That night, I was sleeping in the back room of my mother's flat, and Ibrahim was staying in Peckham. In the early hours, I was awakened suddenly and found myself sitting up in bed, even though my baby was still sound asleep beside me. There was a high hum in the small room as if someone had thrown a switch, and a sort of vibrational current was passing through. The room was alive and dynamic with it. Not a personal presence, a kind of energy, not emotionally or heart connected, but higher, more cerebral and spiritual, clear, direct, and vibrant.

I told this experience to Mrs. Tweedie at our next meeting. Her eyes widened, and she stared at me. "You met the guru. You connected to him," she said. There was a room full of people who were trying to do the same thing. After I told her this, she shut down any further attempt on my part to discover what was happening and why.

I wondered about this and later concluded that perhaps this was a perceived threat to her spiritual authority. She attended to the questions and dispensed answers and life wisdom to the group of followers who came regularly. They were mostly white vegetarian women in their late twenties or early thirties. I discussed Sainsbury's food products with one of them in the kitchen. We agreed that Linda McCartney's new range of sausages was great. Another woman tearfully apologized to us because her two-month-old baby had been crying and "bothering the group." On her way out, she said, "She's usually so good!"

Mrs. Tweedie's group were studying their dreams and doing Jungian-style analysis of their psychological selves to "counterbalance the spiritual states that occur from sitting in the presence of the 'guru' (Satsang) with a highly evolved being," in this case, Mrs. Tweedie herself. She had explained her own process of enlightenment. "What the teacher did mainly was to force me to face the darkness within myself, which almost killed me." Subsequently, when she returned to the West after her enlightenment experience in the Himalayas—described in detail in her book—she incorporated a model of psychological transformation to help the wayfarer understand the inner work of the path. I found this to be a helpful confirmation of the need to integrate the spiritual and psychological models of understanding. Although, in my experience, this often remains a cognitive understanding only and is not a substitute for either therapy or mystical realization.

It is said that strong spiritual states can unbalance the practitioner, and I have certainly seen this—even within the context of Islamic Sufism. Many Islamic Sufis have found practising Islam the most effective counterbalance to Sufism, which can "spin off" into bizarre interpretations of reality. An inner world often operates in an alternative dimension in the same way that dreams do. Time is distorted and different from analog clocks. Place is linked to meaning and significance in peculiar ways. Everyday events are perceived in a different way. These are described by mechanistic, material psychology as psychosis, but the history of these altered states of consciousness goes back to the origins of humanity. In order to remain functional, though, it is necessary to be "grounded" in time, place, and intention, which the practice of the five prayers and other parts of Islam do very well.

At this time, Llewellyn Vaughan-Lee was working on a model of Jungian analysis that incorporated Sufism. He believed there had always been a strong "psychological" dimension, which was in the contents of the "understanding of the nafs." His group, The Golden Sufis, is still practising out of the West Coast of the United States. I remain grateful to him, and his teacher, Mrs. Tweedie, who was a true pioneer and many years ahead of her time.

The Second Trip to Cyprus

༜

W hen the "Peckham Scene" at the mosque in London was no longer happening, we had a dilemma. The only way we could get access to Sheikh was in Cyprus, although the demands on his time and his travels were beginning to take him all over the world. We felt we had lost our momentum and direction in Canada after the failure of the "country project" at Sugarloaf Pond. In addition, our practices felt dry and uninspired, almost like we were losing the radio signal transmission from the tariquat. We decided to go and visit him and stay in Cyprus one December in the early 90s, going through London to visit my mother on the way. This chapter has been made from excerpts from the journal that I kept during the visit.

We arrived on the island at 1.00 a.m. on a Sunday morning. The small airport was deserted as we made our way through customs, waking up the official who waved us through from his chair. We took a long taxi ride through the dark landscape. I felt a strange mixture of fear and excitement, but the taxi was quiet. The two children, who were both under five years old, had fallen asleep. In the quiet village of Lefke, a lone streetlight hung outside the mosque where Ibrahim had proposed marriage many years ago. So much had happened since then. We felt bad about waking everyone at 3 a.m., so we went straight to the guest house on the edge of the village.

When we got out of the taxi with our suitcases and looked at the large building, a considerable change had taken place since our idyllic time there. We had been told by another mureed, when we spoke, to "go straight to the guest house." Did we have the right place? Unpainted, broken wooden shutters were precariously hanging from hinges; some of the panes of glass were gone and had been covered with boards. We thought it was derelict; it reminded me of a London squat. We tried the wooden front door, but it was locked. We asked ourselves, "Is anybody living here?" and then discovered that, yes, they were. After banging repeatedly, while the sky started to lighten, meaning that it was Fajr time, the door was eventually opened by a man wearing a crumpled beige mackintosh with stubble on his face. "What is this game?" he demanded in a strong Germanic accent. He let us in when we explained that we had come from Canada and that Sheikh was expecting us. There was litter and dust all over the stone flagstones and the faint smell of urine. After praying on our coats—strangely, we couldn't find prayer mats—I made my way up the stone steps to the middle bedroom, disturbing an Austrian woman and her son who were occupying the beds. I settled on a couch after putting the children down on rugs and blankets. Exhaustion took over, and we all managed to get some sleep.

I felt shy about seeing Sheikh Nazim again after all the time. He greeted me warmly and said I should go and see his wife. I went inside and greeted Hajja Amina. She kept saying, "Welcome." I was very moved. I thought of everything I had been through since I was last there. The house was more comfortable. There was a stove in the sitting room and a lovely thick prayer carpet in the prayer room off the courtyard garden. I only observed her son using it, though, because Hajja always prayed on a thin little mat.

There were also subtle changes to the family. Hajja Amina seemed sadder and more irritable than before. Rashida also seemed discouraged, moving more slowly and sighing. She had learned to drive a car, a sign of change because, previously, either her brother or another male would drive her and her mother to the market for shopping. We stayed all day because I didn't want to go back to the chaos of the "guest house." It was referred to jokingly as the "ghost (djinn) house," a reference perhaps to the legendary disturbing effects of djinn on the minds of people. I struggled to manage my children, who were confused and uncertain, spilling food on the floor as I was trying to give it to them. As the day unrolled and my presence began to intrude on the business of the household, I started to question whether I should have come.

Someone had built a fountain in the middle of the courtyard. There was no water in it because Hajja was afraid one of the visiting children would fall into it and drown. There had been several incidents with the guest house children, who seemed to be spending a lot of time unsupervised. I was told of one who had been playing in the open drains in the village and been swept away in stormwater. He was later found semi-conscious in a field below the town. I had seen at the guest house that morning a baby under two standing precariously at the top of the long flight of stone steps. It had terrified me, and the mother was not around to intervene, so I did. Even when they were in the same place, their mothers were in a daze and not aware of what was going on around them. I was reminded of Mrs. Tweedie's response to these states of consciousness. They are all too common in many spiritual groups.

There seemed to be a rift between the two women's groups in the village. Each group referred to the other in a negative way. The group at the guest house—the mureeds and disparate spirits who had followed Sheikh back to Cyprus—thought of the women of the Sheikhs family as pampered and materialistic. The more traditional group—the older women who had always lived in the community and the women of the family—considered the guest house and visitors unstable hippies. The younger guest group was centred around Zachra, who now had her own house just down the lane from the zawiya. As Zachra refused to go on the "women's side" and chose to stay on the men's, this had subverted Hajja Amina's authority. Sheikh was pragmatic though and avoided the conflict. He also knew that his wife couldn't stand her. Some of the guest house women had started their own dhikr group, on a Wednesday, another direct rejection of the authority of Sheikh's wife and perhaps to create a space where they could express themselves the way they were used to.

I chose between the groups, aligning myself with Hajja and the women of Sheikh's family, and Rabia, an older European woman who helped me with translation and lent us a small house she had in the village while she stayed at another house on the coast. She agreed we could stay there with the conditions of paying the electricity bill and cleanliness. It was a huge relief and because of this, I was able to have my household and follow the model of the traditional day.

❖ ❖ ❖

I found it odd that the young European women at the guest house, who were all raised in the Western "efficient technical problem-solving mentality," were all behaving in a helpless and "unworldly" way. There was one who would not make any decision without getting the Sheikh's permission, and if she could not get it through direct access to him, would make no decisions at all. She used to wander around the village with her children, pushing her baby in an old pram. Villagers would take pity on her and give them food. The only explanation for some of this group was mental illness or the DSM diagnosis of personality disorder. It seemed that the people on the margins of Western society were the ones who were most receptive to alternatives. Mental illness, anxiety, and depression seemed to be less common in the traditional Muslim circle, an insight that Ibrahim noticed, although they were also present.

The "traditional" women became more empowered and inspired to learn and study Quranic sources. They were very scrupulous about their practice of Islam, and this included the role of women. Hajja believed that women should be married and attending to children, "unlike the single ones who spend their time on the men's side in order to get as close to the Sheikh as possible." She didn't understand the behaviours of guest house "ladies" with their children running all over the place. She was horrified that they got married and divorced so quickly; some marriages lasted less than a few days when the spouses decided they were completely incompatible or just didn't like each other.

This might have been why the guest house group felt rejected, judged, and determined to "find their own way" through their personal relationship with Sheikh. Despite this, whenever women came from the guest house, Hajja always gave them food to take back and tried her hardest to be patient with them. They were a huge test to her personally and publicly.

One morning, I was surprised to find a group of the guest house women at Sheikh's house, on the women's side. Hajja Amina was asking for their help, but they "didn't hear." They wandered or sat while their children threw rocks or fought with sticks. I rounded them up, we gave the children a tub of water to wash vegetables in, and we cut leeks together. We were chopping and cutting vegetables in preparation for important guests who were coming, we were told. Hajja Amina was very busy and was having to delegate and manage the work, which she wasn't used to doing. Normally, she did almost everything herself. Sheikh Nazim came out of the washroom with a pink towel on his head. I remembered my personal practice, which was to focus on the spiritual side of Sheikh, not the Turkish old man.

I asked him if I could study Arabic because I was embarrassed by my lack of knowledge. The work and devotion of the mureeds, the daily round of prayers, were perhaps enough for many of the mureeds, but I always had intellectual curiosity and wanted to understand the Quran. I felt I had to "justify it."

He said, "Yes, why not?" Then he looked at me seriously as I was sitting on the bench by the kitchen, cutting the vegetables and said, "You are free."

I felt jubilant. I had the permission I needed to start intellectual work again, and I also took this as a personal message that I was free to take my own direction in the path of my heart. It was a very important realization for me to have.

＊　＊　＊

Hajja prayed Tahajuud (night) and Fajr (predawn) prayers following the rhythm of an Islamic life. The schedule was that you woke long before the Azan for Fajr, making ablutions, so you were prepared for Salat al Fajr. This precious time was used for reading the Quran (a juz a day if possible) and doing Wird (devotional liturgies). After Fajr, as the daylight came, it was time to stop and go get breakfast. The morning was time to do your work, cleaning, harvesting, cooking, and taking care of the animals. After the prayer in the middle of the day, you had your meal, fed and served everyone around you, and then you rested during the heat.

At the house, Sheikh would come over to the women's side after Salat al Dhuhr prayer and again after Salat al Maghrib. Everything stopped. Hajja would greet him attentively and sit by his side, serving him whatever he wanted—tea, grapes—and they would chat, and he would laugh and joke.

Traditionally, the afternoon, after nap, was the time for visiting and receiving guests, drinking glasses of tea, doing handicrafts and dhikr. Afterwards was family time and then a light supper before bed. There was no entertainment or activities unless it was on the eve of Jumaa, and you were visiting mosques, doing the collective Naqshbandi gathering, or attending a Dars (lesson). Hajja worked unceasingly for the tariquat and for Allah. She was unconcerned by her social status, only her status with Allah. Her humble clothing and natural shyness meant she was often disregarded, overlooked, and even treated with contempt by too many of the people around her husband.

Sitting with the women in Cyprus, though, I often felt restless and anxious, out of place because I was not comfortable enough with myself to just sit. I felt a kind of inner compulsion to earn or justify everything, even my presence on the couch. I felt as if I had no intrinsic right, no heart filled with love and connection through which I was included and connected to others. What these women had—astonishingly obvious and simple and yet so precious—is that they just accepted themselves completely and unquestioningly as they were. They didn't have to present themselves, to charm, to amuse, or entertain.

Part of the reason I think that these women were able to live the way they did—protected, secure, and safe—was because they lived within a caring family in a traditional community where most people knew each other, and courtesy and respect were maintained. If you followed the conventions of the culture, it in turn guided and supported you. You could sit back in your "little velvet box." By contrast, in Britain at that time and while growing up, I saw collapse. Society was in crisis; there was massive unemployment, social unrest, strikes, and breakdown of the economy, of marriages, of families. There were drug overdoses, crime, hopelessness, and the punks. The results of this were clear in the guest house group, who had also left their homelands in Germany and Eastern Europe, amongst other places, in search of stability and care.

It was the hardest thing for me . . . to just sit there. Sometimes, there was a bit of chat; couches were arranged around the walls of the room, so usually, it would be in a low tone between two or three women sitting close to one another. They would talk in a low voice and exchange information and details of weddings, people in the community who were undergoing some misfortune or some good times. This was all conducted in a soft, discreet undertone; there was never any vivacious gossip or loud laughter in ridicule. Mostly, though, it was just companionable silence, punctuated by snacks, pumpkin seeds, grapes, nuts, and small glasses of tea and, of course, the wudu (ablutions), and the Fard (obligatory) and Sunna (preferred) prayers. There was a leisurely rhythmic quality to their days, even with the handwork. It was a bit of crochet or knitting or small embroidery, no feverish factory-style production dictated by goals and productivity.

Years later, when I did a mindfulness retreat, it was amusing to realize that this is what they had been doing all the time in Cyprus. In that sitting, there was a kind of mindfulness. They would notice a smudge on the wall, a fly, not because they were looking but because it came to their attention and that attention was open, calm, and undisturbed. As a child, I observed the older people of the fishing villages in Wales sitting this way, with presence, an awareness of the moment, and a relaxation with the course of events around them. This seems to be a much more natural human state than what we have now with modernization and our constant interaction with devices. At one point, I remember it emerged that a family member of Sheikh was in a bunker near a war zone in another country that was being bombed, and Hajja closed her eyes frequently and murmured a duah or piece of Quran. She wasn't distraught or on the phone to everyone. She just accepted the situation as it was, her powerlessness as a human being to intervene, and trusted completely that Allah would.

I was not the only one who had trouble with the sitting and being. All the Western women did, even the younger ones from more cosmopolitan Muslim countries. I remember a high-status Asian woman who spent most of the time compulsively applying hand cream and, at one point, reached into her bag and pulled out a nail file; however, after she had glanced at Hajja Amina, she quickly put it away again. A gentle smile, a murmur—that was all that was needed to indicate that filing nails was something reserved for private quarters or washrooms and not social circles. Others would get up again and again, visiting the kitchen or bathroom, begging to help. "No, no!" the hostess would deflect, and then we would all sink down into the sofa cushions for another silence until the electronic azan started up, bringing relief—it was time to take our turn patiently to make a wudu that could last up to fifteen minutes while we carefully drizzled tap water over our extremities and murmured the duahs, if we knew them. When I had the excuse of small children who, unlike their Turkish counterparts, were unable to sit still or stay in one place on the floor with a couple of toys. I just avoided this socializing and hurried back to wherever I was based.

❖   ❖   ❖

During this visit, what became clear to me was the complete surrender of Sheikh Nazim to the events taking place around him. I also had the feeling that, in some way, he had lost some personal force since we first met. He seemed less full of joy and light and more burdened by the frequent demands which must have taken him away from his interior life. All the tension and fitnah in the village had somehow veiled the barakah. This situation also mirrored the growth of the tariquat and his branch of the Naqshbandi. The consequences and fallout from the actions of the guests had ramifications for everyone. This was clearest to me in Sheikh Nazim's perception of my "child-raising." He had questioned Ibrahim closely about whether I was "taking care of the children" and when Ibrahim had replied in the affirmative, Sheikh seemed to think that any other difficulties in our relationship were not serious. He dismissed the things that annoyed Ibrahim, such as my sloppy housekeeping, frequent need for socializing with my circle of friends, or evening French courses.

The child-raising issues came to a crisis point when visiting Sheikh's house one time. I had been invited to stay and was waiting for Rabia; it was late in the afternoon. The children—Adilia, then four years old, and Amina, the toddler—were tired and peacefully taking a nap. It was so satisfying to be able to make dhikr and walk in the garden, looking at the delicate flowers and admiring the fruits on the trees. The women started having supper, and although she had napped for a while, I left Adilia sleeping in her carriage instead of waking her up and bringing her to have some food. Amina had woken up and was with me with the other ladies. I heard a car pull up outside, and I got an unusual feeling of dread. Sheikh Nazim came into the sitting room and looked around, frowning and visibly angry. He fixed his gaze on me and said, "Why are you leaving your child out there in the cold?"

It was exactly as cold in the room as it was outside. In a state of panic, I turned to Rashida and asked, "What am I supposed to do? Bring her in?" The light and noise would wake her up and disturb her, and she would probably get very upset. I had also thought she was quite warm enough, as she was dressed in a warm coat and hat. Rashida said to cover her, so I took off my coat and put that on her. Then Sheikh went off into the family quarters and the other guests left rapidly.

I also chose to make a run for it and, on the way out, told him, "I'm taking her home."

He kept mumbling, "She is cold."

I burst into tears, really exhausted and fed up. I was glad to get out of there. As I left, Hajja emphasized that "I was welcome." I had the sense the women felt bad about what had happened.

In reflection, I felt that part of the problem was that I wasn't adhering to traditional time visits, although other visitors had also been there. I was confused about the whole incident and decided to follow a clear routine. In the traditional timeframe at Maghrib, the curtains are closed, and when it is dark, everyone, especially children, is at home in bed. Ironically, in developed cities in the Middle East, it is almost the opposite; social time is at night, and you often see children playing in the dark parks late into the night. That is not the structure that Sheikh was working on; his "Ottoman" attitude also included the routines and behaviours in the family.

After that incident, I managed my visits to the house on a strict timeframe. On arrival, I announced, "I am going to pray Asr, and then I'm leaving." This seemed to work well.

Throughout the rest of my visit, I tried to keep "Sunna time." I worked in the morning, washing, cleaning—dusting and sweeping with vigour—and making large pots of soup, "Peckham style." I resolved to try to ease the situation of tension I was picking up on by helping Sheikh's family as much as I could. I started to cook and take food over so that there would be less work for them. Once, I presented Hajja with small pizzas I'd made, and she seemed so surprised because nobody was giving her anything. After I made Asr, Sheikh Nazim yelled, "Munirah, Doctor is looking for you" exactly on cue. As I was leaving, Hajja Amina gave me some cake she had made in return.

* * *

Once, when I felt unsure whether I should be "bothering them" again on the women's side, I went for Asr and tried to get in on the men's side on the pretext of a question from someone in Montreal. Sheikh Nazim told me twice to go back next door, to the women's side, so I went. Everything was tranquil when I did. We talked about knitting and crochet. Hajja was making a yellow sweater for one of the grandchildren. I was always encouraging her and gave her my Turkish dictionary, which she wanted so that she could learn English. Sheikh Nazim gave Adilia a sweet and told her not to chew bubble gum. I suppose he thought of gum chewing as a bad American habit.

The energy in Cyprus in the sleepy village was strong, however. My sleep was often short, and I had intense dreams. Making midday prayer once, I was transported out of the body into a station of light and then onto a plain of people, all making Sajada with angels overhead and light on light. It was surprising and uplifting. When I finished the prayer, it felt as if the whole room was filled with light. Other times when I was able to make dhikr in the Lefke Masjid, I felt a strong presence descend while doing the recitation. I felt more detached from the world, but not so overwhelmed that I couldn't function clearly.

I was told by someone that when you have intense spiritual experiences and then you "come down" from them, you don't really "lose" them as we may sometimes feel. Instead, you just internalize them as "good karma" or barakat, and they become a part of you. In contrast to this, though, I often felt a knot of black anger in my heart. I decided that this was elicited by my interactions with Sheikh Nazim; my frustration had surfaced from the depths. This may not have been from the situation in Lefke. It is more likely that it was a reaction to multiple events that had taken over my good will. Ultimately, in this intense context, my frustration had emerged in my awareness as such dark anger.

One Jumma, we went to Girne; it was almost unbearable. The women were shut up in a dusty room while Sheikh yelled in Turkish in the main mosque. I had to leave and went up the hill to visit a friend. I felt, *What's the point of any of this?* I didn't really have an amicable relationship with Sheikh Nazim. So, because of this strong, excruciating reaction, I began to tell myself that I must be psychologically unsuited to have any kind of spiritual life. Now I wonder if I was having one of the dark nights of the soul that happen to people while they are doing spiritual practices or if it was just that the guidance I was being given was creating too much conflict in me.

❖ ❖ ❖

One afternoon, I went to ladies dhikr with Hajja Amina's group from the village. We went to a large house, once gracious but now neglected, lived in by an old woman, the last of her line. She lived alone because her family were all elsewhere or dead. The village women met weekly with this intelligent old lady, and they were her circle of friends. This was the social elite of Lefke, and Hajja Amina was their spiritual leader.

For that occasion and often when she went out of the home, Hajja was wearing a little black outfit that looked like a nun's habit and made her look unnaturally severe. There were about a dozen women in various stages of frailty. You could see their white hair and orange hennaed braids under their small cotton Turkish scarves. They had few teeth and deep wrinkles from the sun and their hard lives. The only other European who was tolerated was my friend Rabia, who spoke fluent Turkish as well as several other languages. She kindly translated and interpreted what was going on because I sat quietly in the corner except when I was obliged to recite the Fatihah to prove to them, I was really a Muslim. As a white English woman, they didn't see why I would be and also because this group didn't accept the "guest house" mureeds, there were judgments based on their behaviours and the reality that they were "newcomers" to the village in which these women had lived their whole lives. Many factors contributed to this "us" against "them" thinking.

Rabia explained that the protocol was that the younger women would go around the circle clockwise and kiss the hand of the senior women as a way of showing respect. It was also humbling to show respect to a group of women who didn't appear to have any merit or status in the eyes of the world that I knew. After we both completed this, Hajja, who was seated in the middle, began an animated lecture to the company, who nodded and mumbled in agreement.

"What is she saying?" I hissed into Rabia's ear.

"Oh, she's talking about the misery of Asiya . . ."

"Who?"

"You know, the wife of Pharaoh who was crucified! She's telling them about how much she suffered."

Hajja would evoke the example of pious patient women from the Quran, Bible, and apocryphal sources, such as Halimah R.A. the wet nurse of the Prophet Muhammad (PBUH) or Elizabeth (Isha'), mother of Yahya.[12] There was a kind of courageous resolution in these tales with lots of details of their agonies and their suffering, often at the hands of men but sometimes other women, who cruelly treated and abused them and later brought them closer to Allah and a great place in Jannah. I think the reasoning was the hell of your lives is as nothing compared to what these women went through, and they managed to bear it patiently, so your poverty, your hardship, your suffering and so on is a gift for you. Any tribulations that you have undergone patiently in this life will bring blessing and rewards in the afterlife in Jannah. One of the most elevating things that could happen to you would be martyrdom.

12   Wikipedia, s.v. "John the Baptist in Islam," last edited November 8, 2024, at 04:11 (UTC). https://en.wikipedia.org/wiki/John_the_Baptist_in_Islam

After the lecture, she went straight into the dhikr in a lovely voice and interspersed it with suras from the Quran. I felt sadness at my basic ignorance of surahs and Quran. The only ones most of the mureeds had memorized were the three short surahs we repeated in the dhikr.

They were doing the dhikr with stones. They kept the stones in a little cloth pouch in the room where they became impregnated with barakat. Little Amina tried to eat one, so then I stayed in the hallway. After what felt to me like a long and uncomfortable afternoon, Hajja put her cupped hands in front and made a lengthy duah. Then a jug of water that had been sitting on the side table was drunk and after more hand kissing, we left.

This kind of piety is probably completely gone now. To be grateful for what you have, for whatever crumbs fall your way, and to work and pray unceasingly. Raise as many good Muslim children as you are capable of because life is suffering and temporary. Hope for some comfort and love on "the other side." This dhikr group was probably the only social occasion for many of the women: halal, educational, and spiritually uplifting. It made me feel humbled, decadent, and spoiled all at once. It was a radical departure from the growth-inspired movement, which started a lot of the spirituality of the 60s and 70s. In those groups, the catharsis of your traumas gave you strength to conquer the world and grab everything you could to make your life fabulous and to be loved and adored at the same time, or so the thinking went. This grew into the "you can and should have" absolutely everything you want of the 80s. The Cyprus experience was the complete opposite.

*　*　*

In some ways, my association with Hajja meant that Sheikh was no longer responsible for me. The duty of encouraging my spiritual and moral progress had been delegated to Hajja a little, but mostly to Ibrahim. I accessed the tariquat through my daily visits and by joining in the practices on the women's side. By contrast, the men's side of the tekke was more relaxed, as usual. They were all comfortably waiting there, amusing themselves as best they could. It had also been infiltrated by some of the guest house women, who felt there was "nothing happening" on the women's side, that the spirituality of the Naqshbandi was only around the figure of Sheikh. On the "men's side," however, they renounced any of the respect or status that they had as women and instead became competitors for Sheikh's attention, which was not really appreciated. The behaviour of the men had to accommodate their presence. In the West, this is completely accepted as the way things should be. However, the men didn't have the option to go over to the women's side to access snacks and the garden, and there were more of them.

There is also a fundamental mistake and one that has continued, which is to associate the blessing and benefits of the lineage of teachers with a single charismatic figure. Many could only connect spiritually around Sheikh Nazim; he was the source of all blessings. I found this less and less personally, though. I kept coming up against this figurehead, my Sheikh and guide, who seemed to be living in a worldview somewhere that no longer existed, an Ottoman world of his ideal, which was interpreted as a shining example of the Prophetic message.

❖   ❖   ❖

Sheikh Nazim was polite and kept his distance more during the rest of the visit. After the interactions we had, that was fine with me. I really didn't want to be around him. When he was on the women's side, I just didn't feel comfortable enough to sit with him. He wasn't helping me with my marriage and family, and although he often asked for Ibrahim's psychiatric advice, Sheikh had repeatedly advised him to leave Canada and give up his practice. He seemed to think that all I should be doing was producing lots of male children. If he asked me why I was leaving, which was unusual in a mureed, I would make an excuse, for example, that it "was getting close to Maghrib."

Sheikh Nazim told Ibrahim to buy a house in Cyprus and come and live there. I was furious that Ibrahim would even consider it without consulting me or thinking of the consequences for our children. Although I was managing at Rabia's house, it was very difficult because during December in Cyprus that year, the temperature at night was in the 40s and 50s Fahrenheit. The lack of a washing machine and frequent power outages were not something that I would accept voluntarily. Although this was just part of daily life for many Muslim women in the world, if I had a choice, then I would use it. I pointed out all the discomfort and frustrations we were likely to experience living in Cyprus, as well as the reality that Sheikh Nazim was spending less and less time there.

Fortunately, Rabia, a Cypriot resident for many years, discussed this idea with him, and she was quite realistic about the difficulties. She did not have a family, had a small independent income, and spoke Turkish and Arabic fluently, as well as other languages. It was also obvious, by that time, that Sheikh's advice was not to be followed literally.

❧   ❧   ❧

It seemed to me that the burden of service put on the women was enormous and unfair. I saw how life was for Sheikh's wife and family, who barely got any time with him during his long schedule. Constant guests streaming in and out with demands and needs. Cooking and managing the house on a limited budget and then the stress of the behaviour of the guest house residents was taking a huge toll.

One morning, I made soup for Hajja out of some cow bones and various local vegetables that Ibrahim bought. I stayed at the rental house all morning as I didn't want to visit Sheikh. I couldn't see the point. I wanted her to have the soup as she had mentioned that many visitors were coming on the weekend. Ibrahim took the soup in the evening, and it was served in the tekke. Sheikh had some and said to Ibrahim, "Um . . . very good . . . you are teaching her." In reality, the recipe had come from an English Turkish cookery book I had picked up in Istanbul. I never witnessed any Naqshbandi man teaching his wife how to cook. It was just expected that they would produce the right kind of tasty food whenever it was required. With a wry smile, Ibrahim told me about the comment, and once again, it was infuriating.

❧   ❧   ❧

When all the extended family was there, the sons, the daughters-in-law with babies, it was very domestic and convivial. When Sheikh Nazim came down from upstairs, looking upset, his mood changed to being greatly pleased by news of another pregnancy from a daughter-in-law. It was as if the only thing to look forward to was having more babies, and the best way to earn his respect and admiration was to have lots of them.

Adab—respect, correct relations, and appropriateness—was the rule of social relations in the family. For example, Sheikh greeted all his grandchildren with formal affection and genuine warmth. Traditional cultural Turkish Adab was the model of family relations; everyone knew the expectations and their task. I asked myself if there was something to be learned from accepting and following the natural social order. In terms of the "pecking order," I was pretty much at the bottom of it, anyway.

As a Western observer, though, I found it difficult. I couldn't find a connection with the spontaneity and vitality I had known previously, the openheartedness of the Muslims I encountered when I had accepted Islam on my first visit. Within Sheikh's family, it had been replaced by an Ottoman-style courtliness around the figurehead of the Sheikh. There were rules of deference and superficial compliance covered by smiles and kind words. The roles in my family of origin as I grew up were not defined by the rules of patriarchal social order. I had navigated my own life with few boundaries, social or otherwise. Although this forced me to rely on my insight and instincts to survive, it also gave me a strong sense of people's emotions beneath the surface, even when they were unaware, themselves. All this contributed to the feelings of restlessness and tension I experienced.

I found myself wondering, *Am I on a spiritual path at all? Why do I feel so negative about my Sheikh?* This kept coming into my mind, along with depression and a sense of helplessness. The dark moods were not new. I'd had them as a teenager, and maybe they're hereditary. Stress exacerbates them, and, incredibly, I was experiencing a lot of stress in this little village close to my spiritual axis. It became clear that internal conflict and spiritual aspiration are not resolved by moving closer to a Sheikh or to another country. The baggage and the burdens were not lifted. Rather, they were increased by this stay.

❖   ❖   ❖

One afternoon, after a pleasant visit to the house, I was on the way out with Rabia when we found Sheikh "going through the dustbins," to use her explanation. He was standing next to the fence at the side wall with two metal trash cans in front of him, and it seemed he was carefully evaluating their contents.

He hated "waste" and would recycle stale bread, or order his mureeds to, among other things. He greeted Rabia warmly, and I went forward and greeted him.

"Ah, how are you?" he began and then, pointing at Adilia and Amina, said, "Why is it that you are bringing only girls?"

I should have responded, "Why is it that you are going through the dustbins?" but I didn't because I knew already about his scrupulousness.

I laughed, deliberately not taking this seriously, and joked that Amina was "like a little boy" because she had short hair at that time. Then, I said there was nothing I could do; it was Allah's will, which seemed to be obvious. Tactfully, Rabia suggested that the "next one" would be a boy. Then he looked at Adilia, expressing concern at how pale she was, that she was not fat, and at the same time subtly implying that I was not taking proper care of her. I dismissed this irritably by saying, "The fresh air and the sunshine of Cyprus are very good for her."

He handed Rabia some banana blossoms from the bin and then, finally, something positive, "Yes, very good soup." This, it seems, was an amazing compliment; Rabia was quite impressed. He spotted Ibrahim coming out of the tekke down the lane and said to him, "Go, and help them." I think he meant accompanying us through the village because he wouldn't have meant childcare. Perhaps it also implied go and get busy making babies because it seems like Munirah doesn't have enough to do, she keeps coming to visit.

Rabia said that the game was "whatever you do, you will always be blamed for it." I didn't want any more blame; however, I had already had enough of it. I asked myself, *How am I expected to serve a Sheikh who constantly comes out with such remarks?* If anybody else said that kind of thing, I would confront them. However, from him, I had come to almost expect this, and the consequence was that, in my eyes, he lost credibility. I told myself that it must be progress that I could feel some detachment from this process. If I did not feel guilty or inadequate about what I was doing, then why should I be made to? I had my own moral sense and the capacity to reflect on my actions, and I do not believe that this has made me a defective Muslim or mureed.

Ibrahim was also questioning his place within the tariquat. One evening, toward the end of our visit, he came back from the tekke disillusioned because Sheikh Nazim was making a big fuss about the "important guests" who had come. This was no surprise to me because I had always understood that social status and money put you higher up in the tariquat even then. Ibrahim made duah to have a dream explaining the limited Turkish side of Sheikh Nazim, and then, I had it. There is a special duah called an Istikhara prayer, where you can ask for guidance in any decisions or circumstances. You frame a question or one side of a choice and ask for an answer. If you don't remember your dream or the answer is unclear, sometimes other people close to you receive the reply.

In the dream, I first saw Sheikh Nazim as very powerful and full of light, like in the pictures we all had. Then, he was back in the tekke as a limited human being, addressing the mureeds and saying, "I have failed with you, to turn you into lovers of Allah." Aside from any interpretations of what this meant in a wider sense, I felt the message that we must concentrate on the spiritual body of Sheikh, his connection to higher realms and the chain of masters, not on the physical, human side. If we focused on the "Turkish old man," we would lose sight of him as the successor to Shah Naqshband. The wisdom and light in the core of the tariquat are held within the Sheikh, but it is not a personal attribute or connected with his personality. It is part of a huge spiritual power within Islam. It was important to understand the difference and what we needed to do as mureeds. In principle, we could do that just as well in North America as in his courtyard. At the end of the visit, we knew there was no need for us to be in Cyprus.

❖   ❖   ❖

A few days later, I went to say goodbye to Hajja and the others. I was relieved that I was leaving, going back to London and then to Canada, where my life was and where I had much more choice and opportunity. I had come to feel stifled and frustrated in my role in Cyprus. It took huge amounts of forbearance and patience to be around the "circus of the Sheikh"; and, personally, I didn't see the point. For me, it was more beneficial to do the practices and try my hardest to be faithful to the message of Islam. Despite everything, I still loved Sheikh and his family, but it wasn't necessary or helpful for me or them to live closely. The most significant message that Sheikh had given me was, "You are free." In the time ahead, this was an important reminder that my path was also guided by my heart and my free will.

As I was leaving, Hajja looked into my eyes, and this time, she did not smile. I saw her pain, her heartbreak, her confusion about the way things were unrolling, the whispers and corruption pulling the seams of the tariquat apart. I sighed; I had hoped that she would be apart from it, that her spirituality would allow her to escape from the pain and the heartbreak. This was not the case. She did not separate herself from what was happening around her; instead, she opened her heart, prayed and accepted it. I looked at her, and she looked at me, the girl who was now a mother with her own share of hardship. "Allah Alim" was all she said, and that was that.

"Zero"

❧

During that first Ramadan I spent in Peckham in 1985, there were a few mattresses up in the loft of the old Gothic Victorian church converted to a mosque by the Turkish community. On those mattresses, a few of us camped, including an elderly and eccentric Caribbean woman called Usma, who had appointed herself as caretaker, another American girl who had just arrived, and a tall blonde Swedish woman named Zachra. I was quite in awe of her—a successful model in swinging sixties London who had been on the bus with the Beatles. Although older when I met her, she was still glamorous, wiser in the ways of the world, and recently recruited to the tariquat. She had made the decision to wear only purple, so she became widely known as "Purple Zachra" to distinguish her from any other Zachra, which was unlikely to be necessary.

One morning, we were lying in after a restless night interrupted by prayers, snacks, and snoring from the men sleeping below, and we were talking about our mothers. I was grumbling because I had to take buses and tube trains across London to go and see my mother, who was "drying out" in a hospital somewhere in the vast NHS health system. This happened frequently, and I was often the only person who would visit her. It is also considered a pious act within Islam to go and visit the sick or those in need. I was newly reformed, "doing my duty," and trying to be patient with the situation. This was not fooling Zachra, she told me, as she shared some glimpses of her own situation:

"What I remember about my mother was being a flower girl at her wedding. I think it was her third—there were many weddings—and I was to be the flower girl. And there was this fuss about the dress and my hair and it all had to be just so, you know, and I hadn't even met the man who was supposed to be my stepfather. Of course, when I did, that was that; and so, then, of course, I had to leave, and I came to London."

That I remember this anecdote so vividly is a sign to me that there was a kernel of an important theme for her in this. Perhaps it described a mother who was not emotionally available for her daughter and yet another man she married who would become too interested in the young and beautiful Zachra. The dynamic of beauty and attention from rich men began early, it seemed and had included Gadhafi—"it was only a couple of dates for God's sake, and he was a gentleman!"—and perhaps others whom she was far too smart and discreet to mention.

There were many attempts by Sheikh over the years to "marry her off," but she always rejected them, preferring to remain independent and forge her own path.

The last time I saw her was one evening at the newly bought building in Seven Sisters, London. This was an old convent property that had been bought for Sheikh and about which battles were being conducted, power plays made, and treaties negotiated. It was years after the Cyprus visit, and we went just to see the property because we were in London and everyone was talking about it. We found it; and Ibrahim and I and the children walked around a large brick wall until we found a doorway with an arch and a lit doorbell, so we pressed it. After some time, an inside hallway light came on, and then the large oak door was opened a few inches. In the dim light stood an old woman wrapped in a lumpy-looking beige sweater with a thin Indian scarf over pale grey hair pulled back tightly. It was only when I looked down and saw the flounced purple skirt underneath the cardigan that I recognized Zachra! She had recently been deported from Cyprus and was living there.

"I'm really sorry to hear about what happened in Lefke!" I blurted out. "It must have been awful for you being stuck in jail like that, so unfair . . ." it was only after I'd said it that I realized it was so tactless. However, Zachra simply shrugged and smiled.

The hidden reality of the situation, according to various witnesses and gossips and friends for and against the parties involved, was that Hajja Amina had been completely fed up with Purple Zachra. She had a dominant and continuous presence at the tekke on the men's side, where she had complete access to Sheikh. She was living only yards down the road from his house. Her overall manner of not playing by the usual rules and her direct and "no bullshit" way of conducting herself was at odds with the manners of the family and the village ladies. It had come to the attention of someone that marijuana was being smoked at Purple Zahra's house, and this was, and still is, a big crime in Turkey. Police were tipped off, and Zachra was arrested and thrown in jail, had her visa revoked, and was then barred from Cyprus and her teacher, never to return.

Zachra was customarily gracious and simply deflected my concerns by saying how much work there was for her to do in London for Sheikh Nazim. The new centre was large and needed management, and she had decided that this was her task. That was where she wanted to be now. She had always liked to be at the centre of things, where they were happening, and there were many new and important mureeds and contacts in London. She, in turn, felt sorry for me, peripheral person that I was in Canada a long way from where it was happening. We were very different people with opposite ways of negotiating our life within the Naqshbandi, but we always recognized the value of the alternatives and the wisdom of letting be. We had a mutual respect for each other's commitment to the Sufi way.

We started to chat. Perhaps we both knew this would be the last time our paths would cross, and we sort of wanted to compare notes.

"All he ever does is tell me to have babies, and I've just had my third girl, and I'm not having another one . . ." I admitted.

"Ah," she laughed, "he is always trying to marry me off and get rid of me, you know; it was a joke, a game between us. He calls me Zero, he says to me you are Zero, you are nothing, but you know that is just his way . . ."

This must have been hurtful, but Zachra wasn't deterred. The only way I can understand it was a kind of teasing. A way for him to keep women at arm's length, which was necessary because we were all trying to get as close as we could, some more than others. One of the things I learned early on is that there is no point in even trying to understand anyone else's relationship with any Sufi Sheikh. It is too often . . . complicated.

Zachra had never played the Ottoman game, or if she did, it was in the role of a courtesan, perhaps a haram favourite without the privileges. Sheikh found her amusing and entertaining and seemed to have a genuine fondness for her. Maybe she knew what the rules were; maybe she didn't. Whatever, she was sure enough of herself to stay around her master despite all the rejection and difficulties. Her role as a leader of many of the European and Westernized women was important and significant. She was a voice for their concerns and an advocate of their right to be within the tariquat practices.

"You kind of remind me of Mrs. Tweedie," I said.

"Ay yes, Mrs. Tweedie, my friend. She and I, yes, you know we share an experience . . . how do they say it . . . ? Those who are dancing are thought crazy by those who cannot hear the music . . ."

She looked at me very directly. *Can you hear the music?* she silently asked.

Another Shake Up

❦

One May, in Montreal, I looked in the fridge and checked the cupboard to see which ingredients I already had and what I needed to buy. That morning, I got up early so that I could drop Ibrahim at the metro and use the car to go grocery shopping. We were expecting a lot of guests for the visit to Montreal of the Sheikh's new representative. He was a middle-aged man called Wassim, with a long association in the tariquat; and I had met him and his wife very briefly in Cyprus. We would host him and his visitors in the small bungalow we rented in Ville St. Laurent. I had some onions and carrots in the fridge, and olive oil, spices and basmati rice. I kept piles of pita bread in the freezer.

I had recently met an older, kindly man called Mehmet, who knew Sheikh Wassim from his time in Tripoli. I knew Mehmet had recently started a business venture, a new store a little bit farther from us. I liked the idea of going there because I wanted to make authentic Middle Eastern food for Sheikh Wassim and imagined that, as a fellow refugee and immigrant, Mehmet would have all the right ingredients to prepare this food. There were other ethnic grocery stores nearer, and I loved to do my shopping there. I loved the smell of zaatar and the piles of green coriander, parsley, and lemons. The huge platters of glistening baklava behind glass, wrinkled dates and cardamom-spiced coffee freshly ground and ready to make with a small container of water on the stovetop. Shopping for food in these places was visiting another culture and transported me back to the Middle East, away from the specials and garish packaging at the large chain stores in Montreal.

A gentle, sad man Mehmet had already been through a lot in his life and now, in later middle age, needed to establish a business in Canada to support his family. His new shop was a large retail space, but there wasn't much stock on the shelves. He showed me over to the best produce he had. Large, thick glass bottles of green olive oil. He told me that when the bottom of the bottle was a little bit cloudy, then it meant that this was the best quality olive oil, so I ended up buying one, which I didn't need. I also got some sheep's cheese, some crusty white bread, which was only slightly hard, and he managed to find a large piece of lamb, which I planned on roasting. At the cash register, I told him all about Sheikh Wassim's visit and, as Mehmet had previously said he knew Wassim, I invited Mehmet to come and see him.

I had spent the last few weeks telling everyone I knew about the Sheikh's visit to build support for the intended project of a Naqshbandi centre in Montreal. Mehmet looked at me directly, and he smiled a little. "I just find it curious," he said.

I looked at him, surprised.

"That people like you and your husband, educated people, would consider someone like Wassim as your spiritual guide."

I was a little defensive, but this was not the first time I had been warned by people to be careful around him. With a large and growing Arab-speaking community establishing itself in Montreal, it was relatively easy to ask about people because there were often other people who already knew them.

When Wassim appeared in Cyprus, he struck me as a businessman and an entrepreneur. The word that came to mind was "hustle." I did not think of him as a spiritual guide, or as any kind of replacement for Sheikh Nazim. I reminded myself that Wassim had told us he had been appointed as Sheikh Nazim's representative and from now on, all the mureeds in America and Canada were to report to him directly and not "bother the Sheikh" anymore. I told myself that if Sheikh Nazim had done this, then he wanted us to work with him as much as we could and help him. I told myself that he would be able to make practical suggestions and give some "credibility" to our group, as he was an Arab. One of the issues in dawah was that Sheikh was Turkish, and we were converts and so were frequently seen as both foolish and ignorant. As to the rumours, we followed the guideline that it was always better not to pass judgment on anything based on what is called "waswas"—interpreted as 'whispers of the Shaitain' and meaning negative assumptions and doubts.

Wassim had arrived in America as a refugee and was fleeing terrible circumstances. His wife and family had lost everything and were now trying to rebuild their lives. I felt it was up to all of us, already here, to help him feel at home; hence, the effort to cook familiar food and to try to build the tariquat and support his leadership. So far, Ibrahim and I had gained a small mixed group of men and women who gathered weekly to recite the dhikr and have dinner together. In addition, Ibrahim always provided free counselling, medical recommendations, and referrals. Together, we provided services and hospitality to anyone and their children who came through the door. We saw this as the work of the tariquat which was blessed and greatly needed.

Back at the house, there was a lot to do. I cleaned the lamb, taking off the violet stamp on the side and another green S stamp. I put it into the oven to slow roast so that it would be tender. It was quite large. It would probably be tough, as my other experiences with halal meat had taught me. I only ever bought halal or sometimes kosher meat because I naively thought that the animals would be treated better and that by being bled, the meat would have less of the toxins ingested from the feed.

As it was unclear how many people would arrive to meet our guest, I decided that I had better start in the garden to make it a place where an overflow of visitors could sit outside. It was early summer, and other than the regular airplanes passing overhead to the airport, it was a nice place. We had plans to start a vegetable garden, although we hadn't made much progress. It could probably wait until Victoria Day, the weekend in May when it was safe to put transplants in the ground. There always seemed so much to do and, once again, the lawn needed cutting.

I noticed a bunch of weeds sticking up from a pile of turf. "Tch! There is just too much to do," I said to myself and angrily walked over. I had already observed a few wasps flying around, but it was only after I had yanked one of the plants out that the rest of the nest came to attack me. I dropped everything and ran screaming back into the house, feeling the stings start on my legs, my hands, and my head. Spinning in the kitchen, I was still swatting desperately at the ones that had followed me inside. I had to run to the shower and turn it on full. The chilly water blast did the trick. Pulling off my soaking wet clothes and looking at the puddles of water and squirming wasp bodies on the bathroom floor, I wondered what on earth had happened. Calamine lotion soothed the worst of them, but I counted more than twenty stings. *Has anyone ever been killed by wasps?* I wondered, staring in the mirror at the large welt under my eye and the end of my nose. I sat down to try to calm my shock and do some prayers and the Naqshbandi Awrad. The day was not going very well.

I made brown rice and some lemonade by squeezing lemons and mixing it with brown sugar. Ibrahim and I didn't approve of fizzy sugared sodas, so we never bought them. We drank water and sometimes herb tea cold from the fridge.

I started the long and laborious process of washing the parsley for the tabbouleh, imagining women in small sunny villages doing the same thing, although they probably never had to do it all by themselves like I did. There was only half a bowl full after cutting three bunches of parsley with sewing scissors. Not near enough to make tabbouleh for the more than twenty people I estimated would show up for dinner. I decided to make a sort of vegetable stew, like a ratatouille, so I put onions, a few cloves of garlic, and then eggplant, zucchini, green peppers, tomatoes, and tomato paste together with Hungarian paprika and salt. The fridge was looking empty again.

I opened a couple of cans of chickpeas and tried to make hummus, but the blender made helpless grinding noises, then started to smoke. I was left with some ground peas, some heavy green olive oil, and a layer of lemon juice floating on the top. The pitcher looked like a cross-section of sedimentary rock. Finally, I just decided to tip most of it in the stew, which I did, and then added a bit more salt. I made more basmati rice and put some sesame seeds on top to make it look more appetizing. The children came upstairs from the basement, where they had been playing, and we had some lunch. It was time for their nap after that, but they could not settle, so they went downstairs again.

I noticed out of the living room window that the sunny morning had gone, and now, midafternoon, dark, puffy clouds covered the sky. The maple trees on the street started to wave their branches, and I realized that the wind was picking up. I made some tea and looked at the living room, noting the lint and dust bunnies. I reminded myself that I still had to vacuum and clean the bathroom in preparation for the onslaught of twenty or so men trying to make their ablutions before the prayers. The aluminum windows of the old bungalow started to rattle, a sign that severe weather was coming. I let out a sigh of exhaustion and wished that I had time to lie down, but I didn't.

As I drank my tea, I watched the clouds burst and waves of rain poured against the windows, pushed by torrential winds. There seemed to be some sort of hurricane happening. I heard the water pouring over the roof of the bungalow and then splattering onto the paving at the side of the house out of overflowing gutters. Some drops of brownish water started to drip through the cracks in the ceiling. I got up to fetch a bucket, and I noticed twigs and branches with leaves flying around outside. Then the lights and the stove went off. A huge branch had broken off farther down the street, and the power line lay across the road.

What is happening? The day was getting increasingly bizarre.

As I watched the fire truck and the hydro crew trying to clear some of the debris from the drama, I worried how I was going to manage and when the power was going to come back. The lamb was mostly cooked, the rice was okay, and the vegetables were still crunchy but edible. There would be no tea and coffee, which I felt was necessary to offer guests. It was disappointing, but I hoped that everyone would understand. Perhaps some of the other women in the tariquat would come and bring some food as well. Worst of all, I could not vacuum, so I picked up what I could and tried to brush the dirty beige carpet that had come with the house rental. The rate of drips to the bucket was starting to subside a little.

As I checked yet again on the progress of the street crew, I saw a sleek black Mercedes trying to get past them and then going up on the sidewalk and partly over someone's lawn to get by. We didn't usually see such luxurious cars on the street; it was flashy. I was very surprised when it slowed down and then turned into our modest asphalt driveway.

Abdul Hamid, a large, American-born Naqshbandi, was the first to come in. As a truck driver, he was now the chauffeur of Wassim and had made record time in the new Mercedes. "Salaams," he said, looking around at the gloomy living room and the bucket. Concerned, he looked at me. "Munirah, what's wrong? You look like you've been in a fight!"

Later that evening, the power came on, and I tried to pass the vacuum between the men now seated around on the floor, gazing at Sheikh Wasim as he sat on the couch under the window, the fading light behind him. Back to the kitchen and a new associate, Ahmad, who had run a restaurant, came and helped me. He did some mysterious and amazing blend with spices in the vegetable stew, then sliced the lamb, and laid it out with the parsley on top. He managed to make the peculiar meal look appetizing. The lemonade was not a success, and Abdul Hamid was sent out to buy more pita bread and Coca Cola, which was to become a staple of the visit.

"Why do you serve this food?" Wassim exclaimed. "We eat American food! We have McDonalds and Kentucky Fried Chicken!"

Mehmet also came and made a point of sitting on the sofa next to Wassim and chatting to him in a very undeferential way. He told him about the money I had spent at his shop that morning.

"This is a waste!" declared Wasim, flicking his hand at the others. "These people can fill their stomachs with bread! We need that money for our Naqshbandi centre!"

Mehmet then left, and Wasim proceeded to tell us that he had sold pornography in his video shop in their old country. Ahmad also told me that everyone, except me, knew that Mehmet had a contact at the rear door of Steinberg's meat department, and that was where he bought the meat, which magically became halal after he made duah over it.

The Naqshbandi Franchise

≥

The next morning, a meeting was called for all the Montreal mureeds. As it was during the week, many of them were unavailable, and possibly those that could have come passed it over. As he was now Sheikh's chief representative, Wassim dominated the room on the two-seater couch leaving lots of floor space for the assembly to sit. I, Ibrahim, and the entourage—Abdul Hamid and another man—sat in the living room on pillows taken off our beds. Wassim closed his eyes and murmured as he nervously fingered the beads on his silver tesbih.

"I have an important announcement to make, and it comes from the highest heaven, the resting place of our Noble Grand Sheikh and the awliya of the Naqshbandi in a golden chain going back to our master, the greatest one of all the companions and the first and appointed successor Abu Bakr, Radhio anaaam."

We braced ourselves in awe of what this vital and mysterious message could be, feeling special that we were the ones who had been gifted, chosen, and able to receive it. An expectant hush filled the room.

"As you know, our master, Sheikh Nazim, has appointed me to be your leader and Imam. This is not from myself and not from my ego. I am the humblest of all of Allah's servants and would not wish to have glory and riches in this world, but only in the next."

He looked at us expectantly, and we followed Abdul Hamid's "Ameen!"

"We must build the Naqshbandi tariquat in North America! Every city in America will have the Naqshbandi Centres. We will have dhikr and remembrance everywhere! All the people, the American and Canadian peoples, will have the opportunity to taste our Glorious Way!"

We were slightly taken aback. This was not what we had expected. Since my arrival in Canada, we had been trying to introduce our Glorious Way and had so far met with stiff resistance from all sides. Sheikh Nazim had given the instructions for centres, but this was all very new.

"I have a vision! Everywhere you go in the world, there is McDonald's! Their hamburgers are available all the time, everywhere! Every city, every town, it is there. The Golden Arches. This is their success, their secret!"

"We will be the new McDonald's; we will be the Naqshbandi tariquat McDonald's!"

There was silence while we processed this; but in my own case, the reactive shock and disgust outweighed everything. As an ex-vegetarian and whole-food adherent, this chain was the epitome of everything that felt wrong with the food supply. This was to be our new model and ideal?

"You mean we are going to sell hamburgers? Or halal kebabs?" I asked incredulously.

"No! Not hamburgers! EstaghfirAllah!!"

More silence. The sound of the beads hitting each other.

"We will be everywhere. We will do the dhikr and pray Salat! We will spread the Word of our Noble Way to the whole of the world."

I couldn't say anything. I just didn't get the business model. It was the standard franchise, scaling up, very popular in the business courses of the time. Make a recipe. Trademark it. Sell it as franchise options to everyone, and it was a money machine for the creator. Everything from donuts to hamburgers to . . . er, dhikr and potlucks?

Later, I discussed this with my smart brother-in-law, a recent MBA graduate with an eagle eye on the markets and other opportunities. "Yeah," he said. "It's becoming a little tired now as a model. Many of the buyers of the franchises are bailing under the costs written in for supplies as well as the real estate locations which are rented." He put his head on one side and asked, "What's he selling?" He was as incredulous as I was, which felt reassuring.

❖ ❖ ❖

I would say that from everyone's point of view, the visit was not a success. After we had been received at the Westmount Greystone home of one of the wealthier and hardworking Sufi Muslims, Wassim asked me some questions about the value of real estate in Montreal. He asked what the value of the Greystone would be on the market. He also asked about the market value of storefronts downtown and the value of the other houses we visited. I was puzzled by this interest and wondered if maybe he was going to reconsider moving his family to Canada from California, where they were at that time. Then he asked me to make an appointment for him to visit with our Westmount friend because he was a "very special" person, and he was to receive an enormous spiritual blessing from the tariquat. He also told me not to mention this to anyone.

I was very curious, of course, but after the morning meeting, nothing was said, and I forgot about it. We did not see the man for the rest of the week.

Later, at a different social event, I ran into our old friend again. He did not seem to be very happy and was clearly struggling with illness and old age. I asked him what had happened at his "esoteric meeting" with Wassim.

"Oh," he sighed, "he wanted to know the exact amount my house was worth and how much I had paid for it twenty years ago. He then instructed me to take out a second mortgage on it and give the money to a Naqshbandi centre in Montreal. Why is he driving a new Mercedes when he is asking me this?"

We had all been asked to obtain any lines of credit we were eligible for, and some of the mureeds on government support had been told that they should apply for credit cards, take out loans to donate to the Sufi centre and then, if necessary, declare bankruptcy. Fortunately, no one listened to this command, so it didn't happen.

It became clear to me that Sheikh Wassim was completely serious about his "Naqshbandi franchise" business dream and that we were only the tools and the workers to achieve it. He had become frustrated quickly by the old hippie Mureeds of Sheikh Nazim already in North America because they weren't prepared to align themselves with his model. Many changes were taking place, and most of the old-time mureeds were dropping off, being replaced by the new regime. It was upsetting as many of our friends just left, no longer interested in the Naqshbandi. There were also stories being shared about money and donations, as one ex-mureed put it, "I may not know much about Sheikhs but I know a "shake-down" when I see it happening" None of us ever seemed to know what was happening anywhere else. New people joined the tight group of followers around Sheikh Wassim, those who were willing to make their resources available to him.

Eventually a place was rented on Park Avenue for our Sufi centre, and the tensions within our small group quickly became unbearable as different instructions were given to different factions in a "divide and conquer" policy from the headquarters in California. Sheikh Wassim did not want any other competitors to his position as the controller of access to the Tariquat and its material resources. He gave an interview in a local newspaper announcing that he would buy up some of the church properties in Montreal and make them into mosques. This created conflict locally, as most Montrealers were not ready to accept the loss of their traditional places of Christian worship, even if they didn't use them.

More "secret" marriages took place, and this filled many of the women in monogamous relationships with fear and uncertainty. Now, I realize the threat of polygamy was used as a weapon to keep the women under control. Wassim hinted that I should be very concerned by Ibrahim's practice because he was seeing "attractive women" in his office, behind closed doors. That they were his patients and he was their doctor didn't seem to be understood. Wassim warned me that it would be wise for me if I concerned myself more with "keeping him happy" in our marriage by whatever means necessary. When Ibrahim and I talked about this, he reassured me that this was classic "projection" on Wassim's part.

A small group of us became more and more concerned about what was going on, but we heard fewer details as we were gradually pushed more to the periphery of the neo-Naqshbandi. It was too hard to keep up with it anyway, and we tried to direct our spiritual engagement with other things as a survival strategy.

How to Make Hummus

⁊ℯ

I t was another visit, and this time Wassim had brought his wife along with him. "What is this?" Wassim said, with a frown visible beneath the rim of his turban, the edge of lip lifted beneath his trimmed moustache, above his long beard. We were sitting outside on the cement patio at the old picnic table. As it was during the week, Ibrahim was away most of the day at the clinic, seeing patients. He would come back to the house, exhausted and drained, to a second shift of guests, some of whom were expecting medical advice as well as a meal. In the mornings, the children would go to the jardin d'enfants at the nearby school, but in the afternoons and evenings, they played and ran around in the basement with any other children who were brought along by their mothers. It had been hard to try to get the children to bed with noise coming from the living room and there was only one bathroom, which everyone was using.

On the plastic tablecloth were some bowls with olives, labneh, zaatar, a pile of pita bread, and a bowl of homemade hummus—the hummus he was referring to. His wife frowned, and her lips became a tight line. Her husband was not happy, so she'd better watch out. It had been a difficult visit, and now, toward the end of it, everyone was hungry and tired. I'd laid out what I knew to be a "Turkish breakfast," but also a substitute snack at any time of the day or night.

He spoke to his wife in Arabic, and I couldn't follow it, too fast. He didn't address me, although I was sitting opposite, resting on a hard plank.

She got up and went through the swing door into the kitchen.

She shouldn't be doing that! They are our guests, and for three days, I should be serving them. I hurried to help her find a bottle of lemon juice, olive oil, and the plastic tub of tahini. I didn't offer her garlic, as it isn't a sunnah because the smell can be off-putting for people praying closely in Jamaat. She found some in the fridge, though, so I also brought out the large garlic press. She took the salt from next to the stove, and we both carried out the ingredients, myself, apologetically, because I had triggered his wrath.

He acknowledged his wife seated next to him, snapping his fingers so she passed him a fork. We had no blender or food processor, so he had to use a fork to mash the chickpeas. They were a little hard, not cooked long enough or something. He picked out some skins, dropping them on the table, their translucent bodies lying there on the cloth like the carcasses of insects. The fork pressured down again and again, smooshing the peas. They were supposed to be smooth, fine like flour, light enough to be suspended in emulsified oil added drop by drop. This was "first aid" to make the mess palatable. My feelings often leach into my cooking, and this "hummus" spoke of resentment, disappointment, and exhaustion.

When he had finished crushing, the chickpea mixture was the texture of fine gravel. He snapped again, and his wife handed him the lemon juice. Seeing the bottle, rather than fresh, he frowned. This was not like his own country, where they could pick fresh lemons from the tree in the garden. He started to relax a little as he added a glug.

He now looked over at me, his mood improving. This was a "teaching moment." I could learn how to make real hummus and, more importantly, I could learn how a wife should behave. Referencing the model shown, she should react immediately to the cues from her husband and if a situation is causing him distress, then she must do her utmost to improve it. Specifically, she should never present him with food that is less than perfect! The sad part of this belief is the reality that there is never perfection, only the failure to meet an imaginary standard that keeps changing according to the whims and mood of the person demanding it.

One of my personal reasons for accepting this, or at least trying to "make sense of it," was the Turkish/Arabic version of a "trad wife." This is a modern phenomenon, but at that time, Western women were wearing power suits with padded shoulders and trying to "get ahead" in a man's world. Assuming a "traditional" female role as wife and mother offered an alternative, and it was also the model of the Islamic woman I had learned from Sheikh Nazim's wife. Within many Sufi circles, gender roles were still strict and, within conservative Islam, even more so. If you wanted to be considered a legitimate mureed, which I did, it was important to fulfill the expectations of you and your tasks. I had already received negative feedback on the level of cleanliness of the house from Wassim and had been advised to spend at least an hour a day on daily cleaning, not including laundry and cooking. This was different from Cyprus, where everyone was much more relaxed but more in line with what Wassim was seeing in the large mansions in California.

The other reason that I tolerated it was more neurotic. I was increasingly lost from myself and overwhelmed by daily demands and expectations from small children waking in the night to preparing income tax spreadsheets and receipts. Trying to support and maintain Ibrahim's psychiatric practice as well as "building the Naqshbandi tariquat." I did not "fit in" anywhere. I was a British immigrant into a Quebec culture that increasingly asserted its dominance over all other minorities and generally disliked Europeans. I was following a religious tradition that was starting to be seen as contrary to "Western values." In addition, I had spiritual practices and beliefs that were not understood by anyone else. I was being pulled in all directions and starting to rip. Perhaps if I could simply do what I was being told, then it would all work out?

After mixing the lemon and the salt, Wassim handed the fork to his wife to taste. She nodded and said something. He added more salt and garlic. The garlic came through in small cylinders, dropping onto the surface. He clearly enjoyed pressuring the fat bulbs through the small holes in the press. A smile formed. Then, the oil. The "tasting fork" was also the "mixing fork." I realized this was "their" hummus—it even had his and her spit in it. Did that supposedly give it barakat?!

The bowl was propped up, and the fork whipped around inside it. The oil drizzled into what became a pale-yellow porridge. After whipping again, another taste, then a shrug. A piece of pita ripped off and dunked, eaten quickly. A nod. *Not how it should be, really, but it would have to do. The hostess is incompetent, and this isn't home.*

This was just one personal example of our experiences at this time. Our Sufi tariquat had degenerated into some sort of petty dictatorship. Ibrahim and I were less and less recognized and valued in this regime. We really did not know what would happen next. I had already witnessed lies, gross exaggerations and outright manipulation in the service of "building the tariquat." Worse, there was no spiritual benefit in any of the practices or gatherings. They felt like we were at a fundraising dinner without the food or the entertainment.

Ibrahim decided to go on a quick visit to Cyprus to ask Sheikh Nazim about the situation. To what extent was he involved, and had he really "signed off" on all this? He had a meeting with Sheikh Nazim where things were said. It is not my place to report them. In summary, Sheikh Nazim was not prepared to intervene in what was taking place. Perhaps he saw it all as "the will of Allah"; perhaps it was. After a few days in Cyprus, Sheikh Wassim appeared. After that, Ibrahim no longer had exclusive access to his Sheikh. It was a turning point in the relationship, though, and now we were definitely on the outside.

We heard from others that Sheikh Nazim would come to North America to attend the wedding of a family member. As our loyalty and love were still with him, we packed up the car, me, Ibrahim, and the children, and headed down to the States.

Woodstock Visit

꒦

Long before the news media made Islamic terms familiar, the people of Woodstock, NY, were invited to accept the Naqshbandi Way and become Muslim. We all followed behind Sheikh Nazim on his first visit to the USA at the beginning of the 90s. He walked regally with his cane and turban through the streets of Woodstock village. Gradually, more people saw him and joined the procession. The march swelled as we walked. I remembered a picture of the Pied Piper of Hamelin from one of my childhood storybooks. Like in the story, the music played was invisible to the ears of the "adults"; it was only heard by the "young at heart." This being Woodstock, the crowd that was attracted was curious and interested in this figure and what he had to contribute to their alternative lifestyles.

It had been a difficult trip for us thus far because access to Sheikh had been obstructed by the itinerary and his American gatekeepers. Since his arrival a week before in New York, there had been sightseeing—the Statue of Liberty and Staten Island as well as a visit to the Jerrahi Mosque in central New York. Sheikh Nazim and Hajja Amina had been brought over to publicize the Naqshbandi Way and meet influential people who could facilitate the growth of the movement.

One of Sheikh Wassim's representatives bluntly told us that we "had had our time with Sheikh Nazim" and that "we should leave and go back to Canada." After our dissatisfaction with the new order was made clear, we were perceived as no longer useful. We persisted, though, because we really wanted Sheikh Nazim and his wife to come to Montreal and visit with us. We all believed that because of our long-standing devotion and promotion of the Naqshbandi Way, he would accept. Sheikh Nazim had not refused, and we believed that he cared about us and that we mattered despite all the signals we were getting from his entourage. He had personally greeted me warmly on his first arrival and was happy that Ibrahim and I were around as well as others from Montreal.

I was very fortunate, though, because I had mentioned to someone with influence that I wanted to do an interview with Sheikh for a New Age magazine. The editor had given me the "go-ahead," so all I had to do was find the opportunity. Wondrously, it was decided that I could do the interview in the village hall of Woodstock in the afternoon, when Sheikh Nazim was to be introduced and the residents of Woodstock would be invited to meet him.

There were many people living alternative lifestyles in Woodstock, and a sizable portion followed different gurus and were familiar with Eastern and Western spiritual practices. The things that united them were the rejection of organized religion, which was considered obsolete, and the embrace of mystical experiences. On the surface, the general perception of the Sufis was broad and positive. My experiences with Michael's group in Schweibenalp, when I first encountered Sheikh Nazim, had taught me, however, that many of the older hippies were the most closed-minded when it came to the Islamic part of the message. On previous occasions, I had observed Sheikh's representative deliberately downplay and minimize the Islamic component to broaden the appeal base. I wondered if Sheikh Nazim would compromise in the same way as previous Sufis, such as Idris Shah and Hazrat Inayat Khan, had.

Sheikh Nazim was the ultimate performer. He always read the room. As we sat on the stage together in the village hall, I watched his blue eyes move around the crowd, making contact and sensing who they were and where they were "coming from." My hands shook a little as I turned on my tape recorder and placed it on the wooden floor between us. Sheikh Nazim turned to me, his "set-up," and nodded. It was my cue. I made a short duah before I started my introduction with "Bismillah Erahman Eraheem."

As I checked the small red light showing the recorder was on, I noticed that Sheikh Nazim's grey worsted wool cloak looked like it had just come back from the cleaners. One of the things that was subtly marvellous was that even when he had been wearing the same clothes for days on end, his clothing always seemed to have a "back from the cleaners" sort of glow. It was nice to see him back in the more sombre grey because, at one point, he had been given some purple-striped clothing, which was flashy and out of character. The turban and beard were enough of an attention grabber, so that grey and more muted colours added dignity.

I introduced him with exaggerated reverence because I wanted the audience to understand that this was not just another "spiritual entertainment" show passing through. We needed to establish the concept of the Noble Naqshbandi tariquat, as we then referred to it, and "The Way of the Heart", which was the euphemism for our practice. The objective of this was to try to get as many people as possible signed up and into the tariquat. I always understood that the goal was to initiate as many as possible.

Although Sheikh Nazim was incredibly charismatic, he never made himself the subject of his discourse. If a personal anecdote was necessary to illustrate a point, he always used "we." Another remarkable feature of his discourse was that it was always "off the cuff." He might have made "mental notes," but I never saw him refer to paper notes or even texts. He relied on inspiration, linking himself with his teacher, Grand Sheikh Abdullah Daghestani. At times, this was more obvious than others. His emotions showed strongly when he was getting a firm message. The "Grand Sheikh downloads" (spiritual messages and insights generated from his link to his own Sheikh) had become increasingly fierce and sobering over the years I was hearing him. In his opening statement, he referred to his Silsila, the heavenly spring from which his inspiration came.

"The Naqshbandi order is a way of making people reach heaven, and it needs, firstly, training. It is the most famous and distinguished way to make a connection for people with their heavenly stations."

"How can a person become an electronic engineer through eighteen words or in a few minutes? I may say only that if a person is asking to reach that connection with the spiritual world, he needs a master. Master must be. When you find a master, then he should train you to reach any station through heavens. When I say 'stations,' that means that master who is authorized to take people to that level, his authority is going to be in limits according to his spiritual rank, spiritual authority and spiritual power."

As he described the process, it made me reflect a little on the "training," the "jihad al-nafs" I had been receiving lately. I had spent over a week trying to manage my own young children and some other people's as we changed locations and drove around, pursuing Sheikh's entourage. I just got increasingly tired and irritable. My prayers were frequently calisthenics, which left me even more exhausted and were often interrupted by my mind scanning the environment for dangerous activity from the youngsters. Where was the inspiration and ecstasy that I had known prior to my involvement with this movement? Was this training only for people close enough to the Sheikh?

I thought of my time with his family and the Cypriot community and what I had seen there. In the devoted mureeds, I had witnessed the grinding away of the sense of self and the drudgery of unacknowledged service, the "jihad al-nafs." Was this really what a "jihad al-nafs" actually meant, or was it just a role that was part of a simple traditional culture? I was ashamed that I felt envy for some of the "non-Naqshbandi" female entrepreneurs who had thriving import businesses and small shops. Why had I allowed myself to be put into the position of a medieval Ottoman peasant? Did I believe that the expectations and demands for service to the tariquat that I had placed on myself meant that I had to disregard my well-being and that of my family?

Worse, I had not seen anybody "graduating" from the Naqshbandi movement. I had yet to meet the "spiritual electronic engineers" who, after years and years of doing practices, had "succeeded" in the program. One of the most experienced mureeds I knew, who had lived in Cyprus and spent a lot of time with Sheikh, had recently decided to return to North America with his second wife. He had disappeared into a community in New Mexico. We had repeatedly tried to work with the North American "CEO", Sheikh Wassim, who only demonstrated a strong entrepreneurial mindset. This was all making a kind of black hole in my spiritual worldview.

In an effort to direct the interview for both the Woodstock audience and the magazine, I asked Sheikh about what he thought of the "pre-Millennial New Age" belief in the evolution of humanity and the dawning of the Age of Aquarius where we would all live in peace and harmony. It was a popular philosophy at that time and made better holistic sense than simply scientific and technological materialism, which was becoming increasingly dominant. He raised an eyebrow and became curious.

"They are wanting to live like angels?"

Later, this made me reflect on my own tendency to try to "space out" of conflicts and difficulties around me. There was a wish to transcend the suffering and difficulties of this world and escape to some "higher place of consciousness," where I wouldn't be disturbed. It also described some of the ethereal "spacey types" I had met along the way. In Islam, we believe in angels, which are made of light, Nour, and don't have a gender. They are also unable to make their own decisions, as they are the complete followers of the divine decree. It is not possible to live as an "angel" because humanity is made of clay and embedded on the earth. I also wanted Sheikh to address the increasing belief that humanity was evolving into a more spiritual and harmonious way of being because I wasn't seeing it. He gave a better and more informed response.

"Mostly, people are fed up with atheism. There is now an opposite current growing up against it. Our souls are getting more and more interested through their improvements. Atheist people, they are cursed people, they are devils. They can't give people peace, and people are looking to find it and beginning to ask ways to find contentment through their souls.

"There may be such a group of people who heard that someone, through rockets, is reaching the moon, but they are not knowing how they reached from where they are beginning, and they begin to ask the way to reach the moon, knowing that people are reaching peace through their inner lives, through spiritual ways, but these not knowing exact method or system that people are using to reach to heavenly stations and as I said I am not yet meeting them. You know them?"

I agreed that there was a lot of interest and curiosity about the many different and diverse ways of being. An important part of any alternative setting is the "bazaar" of spiritual offerings and methods, the colourful and unique ways that they have of accessing the divine in many languages and cultures. My personal worldview and the beginning of my spiritual journey started with my introduction to the religions of the world.

In my eyes, the fundamental difference between the New Age, Hindu, and Buddhist practices was the holistic nature of Islam. There is an Islamic perspective on every aspect of life. It provides grounded clarification on the "right way" to do things from birth to death, to starting a business or raising a family. This makes it a distinct cultural force to the usual way of American living, working, and consuming. The Islamic emphasis of the tariquat was also something that I wanted to bring in because, for me, it had been something that was initially seen as an obstacle to illumination and which I had later understood as a support. There were also the numerous "cultural practices" that were attached to the Islamic way of life. Sometimes, I could not see why I should follow the rules of a culture that seemed to me in a liberally educated mindset as "backward" or "unfair". It was time to confront the turban in the room.

"People like Sufism, and they love the Sheikh, but they are not sure about whether they want to be Muslims. You are practising Islam. What do you have to say about this?"

"They must leave their imaginings," he said. "(i.e., their negative perception of Islam is due to their imagination, not the truth.) Islam is the best. Islam is the purest way. If they are not accepting Islam, they are never reaching any (spiritual) station. It is impossible. Who is reaching any station without coming to Islam? Come to me! Show me! I am a spiritual person, I know everything."

"Those claiming to be spiritual, where are they? Who is claiming to be a master without practising Islam? Who is that one? Who is that brave one? Must come to me! Show himself!"

I blinked and checked my reaction when he said this. I was surprised by how direct he was. There was no subterfuge in his message and no accommodation of the diverse and very liberal mindset in the room. I observed the shifting in bodily positions as some of the audience began to get out of their "comfort zone." No one came forward in response to this, even those who were following gurus who were claiming God consciousness. Instead, they stared at him, and he stared back, utterly confident in his righteousness.

Now, years later, I am reminded of Muhammad Ali before a fight, affirming that he was the greatest and would absolutely beat any contender. I do not think this was just a psychological strategy. As I was living it at one time, Sheikh Nazim was great and the best of spiritual choices available.

His voice rose as he continued, the speech speeding up and grammatical mistakes coming with the urgency to get his message across. The audience was riveted. The cameraperson for the local television station came in for a "close-up."

"Not in heavens, but mostly underground, not reaching up but running around underground."

He compared other spiritual teachers and their followers to rats, living underground, following tunnels and unable to see the light.

It was important to me that we establish the plurality of religious beliefs in North America. As well as a pillar of democracy, I felt it was important that the Naqshbandis take a place of mutual respect and make alliances with the other monotheistic traditions. They should also understand the broad appeal of the meditative techniques of Eastern religions. I had previous experience with some of these practices, and they had helped me personally. Once again, I struggled to accept this singular version of the world. It didn't make sense to discard huge amounts of human civilization because they don't fit inside our worldview.

Politically, Sheikh Nazim also had some unusual opinions. He was a fierce monarchist and believed in the divine right of kings, the influence of the Ottoman Empire. He also was ardently opposed to communism, which many of the tariquat had fought against in various wars and uprisings. There was a line of Daghestani warriors in our branch of the tariquat. In some ways, the libertarian message of the USA was compatible with the Naqshbandis.

Sheikh Nazim also had a distinct sense of what the "real Islam" was. "Islam is something," he said, "and living Muslims, they are something else. Why are they looking to Muslims living in our days—why they are not looking to pure Islam? . . . I am not asking them to imitate our Muslims living nowadays. I am not happy with them. I am Muslim, alhumdulillah, but I am not happy from Muslims. They are not keeping real Islam; that is the point. I am angry with Muslim world, Muslims, all of them. Their ways are wrong now because some of them Eastern people's ideas—some of them following, imitating Western countries. They are not keeping original Islam.

"This is why people are seeing the Muslims and saying, 'No Islam.' I am sorry, they are not going to be like the Prophet's (PBUH) companions that went through East and West, and people loving them, respecting them, accepting them. Muslims must represent love, respect, mercy, and justice. They lost it, even among themselves, they finished."

I sensed his frustration and sadness with the Muslim world. In North America, it was dominated by the Wahabis from Saudi Arabia and their fundamentalist, oppressive message. The subtle smell of rose water came and he raised his arms and cupped his hands, a sign that he was petitioning Allah.

"I am asking from the Lord Almighty Allah to send new blood. Awliya, maybe. To fill the hearts of the Muslims again so that others may see Islam as it is."

In my mind, I had imagined a soft, cozy, and liberal speech, projecting his warm sense of humour and goodwill. Schmoozing the audience with the message of love and compassion and the "Mercy Oceans" in the books of his talks from previous years. I yearned for the love, affability, and contentment that came with sitting in sunlight, reciting the tesbih, and hearing a rooster crow in the distance in the village. There was none of that now.

As questions came from the audience, the interview unspun into political debate and a mild confrontation when someone tried to call out the exact methods for spiritual transcendence the tariquat was practising. I changed the tape in my recorder, but it was hard to hear the questions. As far as my participation went, it was over. As a last comment, Sheikh Nazim thanked Sheikh Wassim saying that he was a humble one and was serving the tariquat, not himself.

I had wanted to share the wonder and mind-opening experience of the Naqshbandis, to show the audience a glimpse through the Ottoman doorway. I do not think this was the view the audience got. Later in the trip, the Sheikh was taken around Disneyland, making him look like he had stepped out of a cartoon version of the Arabian Nights. These actions made his message seem "quaint," entertaining and ultimately irrelevant.

After the interview, one of the Woodstock mureeds told me, "Sheikh says Munirah will write a book" At that time, it felt ironic because I didn't have either the time or the publishing experience to dream of that possibility. I was too busy trying to survive, raise my children, and keep a home together. I was living in Quebec, where the dominant language was not my mother tongue, a familiar experience for nearly all of the immigrant women there, also publishing in English Canada was not part of my world.

At the end of the interview, Sheikh had looked at me and said, "Munirah, are you happy?"

I had said yes because for the first time in many years, I was. I felt so fortunate because I had been able to ask my own questions without interruption and to sit in the company of my Sheikh. I was doing what was most meaningful and I was resolving some of the issues that had troubled me. I hope that in doing so I was able to clarify some things for the audience also. He still comes to mind when I read this and he is smiling.

The interview formed a full circle from my initial meeting with Sheikh in the pine chalet. On this first visit to the United States, he had presented a shocking and radical stance for the time. In the aftermath, I began to question more about what I was involved with and promoting. It became even clearer to me that the Naqshbandi tariquat in this form was unlikely to be accepted within the New Age movement, recognized as an alternative and interesting way of being in the world among many. It was rejected by the "hard-line Muslims" as well as young professional Muslim immigrants, who had replaced traditional piety for economic striving in their "new country." The tariquat and its worldview needed to be "rebranded" and changed to reach a wider group and, eventually, it was.

Understandably, the New Age magazine refused to publish my piece, and a nonfiction writing teacher said later that "he was running rings around me," and I should have been much more confrontative. The sense among the inner circle was that it was a triumph, though, because it had received coverage and viewers on the local television station. There was little knowledge about traditional Islam and this was well before the events that shook the world on the eleventh of September and the consequences.

The Abode of the Message

❦

All we wanted was to sit in the company of Sheikh Nazim (sorbet). By the end of the week of his Woodstock visit, it became clear that lots of other people wanted that as well.

We waited all morning in the Jeep by the side of the road outside the house where he was receiving people. The children were once again in their car seats and squirmed miserably. I took them out several times to walk them around, and we found a small park a little way up the road, which was a relief. All the Montreal delegation had been told that they were not to go into the house to be with Sheikh to "give time" to the Woodstock people and others who wanted to know more about the Sufi Way. We accepted this because we were still hopeful that our petitions would be heard by Sheikh Nazim and that he would come up to Canada before he flew off to California. Wassim had already decided that Montreal was not "on the agenda" despite the active presence of our group there.

Hajja Amina sent out a gift bag for me containing a small cabbage-shaped teapot and a cup and saucer. Someone had given it to her, and so she passed it on to me. This might have been because I was British or because she appreciated the interview, which I had done a few days earlier.

At last, the door opened, some of the bearded and turbaned men came out, and then the smiling Sheikh. He was quickly ushered into a large black SUV, and the rest of the family went into another one, which was following right behind.

The tinted windows gave the whole thing a sinister look, but we were used to that by now. The rumour was that they were leaving Woodstock and heading north.

I was still hoping that they would drive up to Montreal, an eight-hour trip from there. The Montrealers who were still present were hoping that as well. There was a "Sufi centre" now on Avenue du Parc, and there were regular gatherings every week. There was a significant-sized group of Naqshbandi as well as tariquat-minded Muslims in Montreal, and I knew it would be a huge boost to them if they could meet him there.

As the cars sped off and onto the freeway, it immediately became clear that there was no expectation that any other cars would be following behind. The older cars of the regular mureeds were unable to keep up. I had a strong hunch that the intense speed was quite deliberate. We were not welcome to come along, and we were expected to go home to where we had come from. It was a snub to all of us and created a lot of disappointment, but the message was clear.

The next few hours I spent scanning traffic ahead to spot the black Escalades as they weaved in and out of the other traffic on the freeway. A young man had taken over the wheel and was driving as if he were in a video game car chase. I alerted Ibrahim to whichever lane they were in or to which exit they were heading. The children dozed off as the miles continued. Every now and then, the cars pulled into a stop for wudu breaks or boxes of Kentucky Fried Chicken delivered through the back windows. I wondered if Sheikh or Haja Amina was eating it. We didn't stop for prayers, though, which was strange. In the Shafi mezheb, they are combined when travelling as it is considered too much of a hardship to delay the journey, but Sheikh Nazim followed the Hanafi interpretation, so they must have been made up later.

The real hardship, however, came with the realization, in a dirty garage washroom somewhere in New York state, that my children were neglected and suffering from the days and days of this trip. As I wiped them down with baby wipes, I realized I was putting everything that I cared about on hold while I chased after a celebrity Sufi who was now out of my world. I was the spiritual equivalent of a groupie on a rock star tour, except that I was of "no use." It was hard to accept that I had been "dumped." Ibrahim was more tenacious and refused to submit to Wassim's control. He knew that Sheikh Nazim had insight and a wise heart and was still loyal to him. At that point we imagined that the strength of our connection to Sheikh would mean that somehow, we were out of the sphere of control of Wassim.

The new order in North America under the stewardship of Sheikh Wassim and his family was clear. The richer the people, the closer they got to Sheikh. The bigger the house, the more likely it became a location for a visit. There were even "security people" for the ladies of the family, taking the place of personal servants and making sure that no one had access to them.

Ibrahim managed to get information from an old tariquat friend that they would be heading to the Abode of the Message[13] in New Lebanon, New York.

The place name sounds like something out of Tolkien, and it was, at that time, a bucolic landscape peopled by otherworldly characters. A commune cum ashram housed within the structures of an old Shaker community in the beautiful landscape of the Berkshire hills in New Hampshire. New England was the original launching place for several non-conformist religious movements, like the Quakers and the Shakers, who influenced the American religious and spiritual landscape for many centuries. It was particularly appropriate that Hazrat Inayat Khan chose this place as the North American Centre for his Sufi movement and that many years later, it still survived to bring the Sufi message to us.

It was a place of sanctuary and a place to simply be. I felt that and such refreshment when we arrived in the Jeep and looked through the rolled-down windows at the stately mature trees in the woods around us. We had spent hours in the car. Ibrahim was happy also. It was the place where he had started his spiritual search, attending Sufi camps in the 1970s and listening to Pir Vilyat Khan, the successor of his father, Hazrat Inayat Khan.

We were both relieved that, finally, this tour was bringing Sheikh Nazim to a place of genuine spiritual teaching as well as an inspiring natural landscape. A place that connected to the lineage of Sufism in the West and that had welcomed many young people over the years. I was lost and uncomfortable in a world of flashy real estate and luxury cars.

With a sigh of relief, we unloaded the kids and breathed in the pure, clean air. The afternoon light was gentle, filtered through the leaves, and all the various children played together in a grassy meadow, running and laughing for the first

---

13   Wikipedia, s.v. "The Abode of the Message," last edited October 27, 2023, at 11:56 (UTC). https://en.wikipedia.org/wiki/The_Abode_of_the_Message.

time in days. I felt at peace as we did our noon and afternoon prayers collectively; afterwards, I tried to make sense of the events of the past few days.

I felt at home at the Abode. I thought to myself how wonderful it would be if any Naqshbandi centre that we might have could be like this one. It was communal without being cult-like and free-spirited in the sense of tolerance without being permissive. In the words of the founder of Gestalt therapy, Fritz Perls:

I do my thing, and you do your thing.

I am not in this world to live up to your expectations,

And you are not in this world to live up to mine.

You are you and I am I,

and if by chance we find each other, it's beautiful.

If not, it can't be helped.[14]

We spent a beautiful afternoon in the community. The people around there were old-style hippies who had gone from Haight Ashbury to the Sufi Order of the West with Hazrat Inayat Khan.

When Sheikh Nazim arrived, once again, the entourage was whisked behind closed doors. After what seemed like a long wait, we were told to walk up a hill along a gravel road to a large marquee pitched on the brow of the hill and surrounded by dense woods. The Sheikhs, Nazim and Pir Vilyat Khan, came up in a golf cart and then settled into two chairs on a dais in the centre.

As I gazed at Sheikh Nazim and Pir Vilyat sitting together in front of us, it was like those precious first teachings in Schwiebenalp, and I thought, *This is perfect. It doesn't get better than this.* The moment rolled out like a carpet of flowers and there was light and love and my beloved Sufism.

At one point, Pir Vilyat rose majestically from his chair and did a whirling dervish turn in honour of Sheikh Nazim's mother, who had been a Mevlevi. It could also have been that she was raised in a Mevlevi family because it is unlikely that women whirled at that time. He turned awesomely, and we watched, spellbound. Adilia jumped up before I could stop her and ran toward Sheikh Nazim, pointing and saying, "Did you see what he did? Did you see that?"

Everyone laughed, and the two sages smiled. At that time, whirling was not part of the "Naqshbandi thing" and had never been a part of previous Naqshbandi groups. It was later added to the Western Naqshbandi menu, and it

---

14   Fritz Perls, "Gestalt Therapy Verbatim," 1969.

has become much more popular as a practice in the West. It is also promoted as a "cultural dance" by the Turkish government.

Shortly after this, my youngest one started getting restless. There were some nasty looks and a visit from a "security guard" from the Escalade. She hissed that my children were disturbing the meeting, so I took them outside. Families and children were not welcome anymore, and this was consistent with the neo-Naqshbandi model.

I sat outside the marquee entrance flaps, trying to listen to what was being said. I had some snacks in my enormous cloth bag and gave them to the children, as well as trying to nurse the younger one. After some squirming and head-turning, she settled for a juice box. We marvelled at the dark silhouettes of the trees and listened to the crinkling leaves and chipmunks. An owl hooted in the distance.

Suddenly, from out of the tent came a tall, imposing figure in a white robe. Pir Vilyat stared at me, and his eyes seemed to be blazing. I have never seen a look like that before or since. I wondered if he was angry. It was literally awe-inspiring.

"What are you doing here?" he demanded.

I searched my mind for an explanation and took the most obvious one.

"My children were making a noise, so I brought them outside."

He repeated the question, clarifying it, "What are you doing here . . . with them?"

I just stared at him, not getting the implications or the context.

He raised his voice as you would to wake someone up. "You are a Sufi!"

Then he turned around and paced rapidly back down the hill along the forest path.

Years later, on another visit to the Abode, I told this interaction to one of the long-time residents, and he chuckled. "Oh yes, Pir was pretty disgusted by that visit. Showing off in their flashy cars with their handlers and telling the world that this was Sufism. It was more of an attempted coup than a genuine Sufi meeting in his mind. Maybe he saw that you were more suited to our way."

I also heard that Sheikh Wassim had tried a "takeover," telling Pir Vilyat that he should hand over the Abode to the Naqshbandis so that "real Sufis" could once again have a base in North America.

Pir Vilyat Khan and Sheikh Nazim at The Abode of the Message, New Hampshire

The Fall, the Falls

❧

There was a photo of us taken beside the Falls. The only photo I have of all our family with Sheikh Nazim was taken at Niagara Falls. Nearly always, Ibrahim and I were on separate sides, and later, when the children were present, I was often somewhere else, taking care of them. There were so many people around Sheikh it would not have been possible to get a picture like this—yet here it is.

We spotted Sheikh Nazim alone, sitting on a rock ledge looking at the Falls. There was a large pool eddy in front of the iron railing protecting us from falling in. A faithful Montrealer called Jonathan suggested we sit for the photo; it would not have occurred to us to do so. I also intuited that we were interrupting Sheikh in the first solitary time he might have had in many days.

In the photo, Ibrahim still looks determined and optimistic. Adilia sits on her father's lap. She is gazing far away out of the picture, away from a place she does not want to be in, back toward familiarity and home. I see how exhausted and sad I was, knowing we had failed, that we had been pushed aside. Despite the positioning, Sheikh Nazim cannot be at the centre of our lives. Amina on my lap looks mad and rebellious. She had been stuck in the car seat for too many hours, never stopping as we pursued Sheikh through the States. We had a cooler in the car, and we had lived off bagels, cream cheese, tomatoes, and fruit.

145

Just after it was taken and Jonathan handed the camera back to us, Ibrahim pointed to the towers, Ferris wheel, and casinos of the Canadian side, much more built up and developed than the gentler American side where we were.

"Sheikh Nazim, please, come to Canada!" Ibrahim pleaded, pointing toward it . . . "Look, it is right there!"

Sheikh Nazim frowned. "What for then? What is there in Canada?" he answered with unusual gruffness.

He must have been told things we were not aware of, a narrative of what was happening that we did not know about. Backroom agreements had already been made. The game between the old order and the neo-Naqshbandi franchise was over. We had lost.

"What is in Canada?" Ibrahim said, shocked at this point. "Your mureeds!!"

The last time I was in the physical presence of Sheikh Nazim, Niagara Falls (1991?)

The effort of the last years tumbled down, like the Tower of the tarot. We would not be able to bring Sheikh Nazim to Montreal for a visit. He was not "our Sheikh" he had been taken over. There was no "fruit tree rustic commune," no enlightenment breakthroughs. Instead, a constant struggle between egos and power trips between California and Quebec, between a business and a mystical path and large personalities at our rented "Sufi centre" on Park Ave. We had hoped that a blessed visit would give direction and confirmation to our small group, that his presence would make everything right like a fairy grandfather.

Sheikh Nazim stood up and said "Al Fatihah" in a whispered voice, cupping his hands, and we joined in, but he finished before we did and turned away.

He carefully climbed the stone steps toward the black Escalade, which had pulled up again, waiting for him. An inner intuitive voice told me that this was the last time I would see him. My mind reacted, *No! That cannot be true.* I panicked at the thought of losing him and pushed the thought away, imagining that the directions would change, and all things would be as well as my heart wished.

He is my touchstone and my guide. I have built my life and my family around his presence, the central pole of my spiritual and material life. He hunched and did not look back as other hands pulled him up and through the car door. My last image in this world was with his back to me.

This had not been a vacation, despite the "sightseeing" trips and so on arranged by Sheikh Wassim and paid for by a rich new mureed who would soon have to pay for even more. The inner circle was wealthy newcomers to the tariquat, while a few old timers served in menial positions. The new people with financial resources would donate to the new business that will replace our old tariquat, our Sufi brotherhood. This will make the Sufi franchise.

Later, a community would be started in Michigan, close to the Ottoman ideal. There was an all-powerful ruler and leader, his family, and advisers and then the serfs who would do the work, occasionally getting assembled for celebrations and honouring the leader.

We had been told that to be a Naqshbandi mureed, you should follow the Sheikh devotedly. It was impossible to do that. The organization had expanded rapidly; the work had been delegated. There were branches throughout Europe, Malaysia, and Asia. North America had been "given" to Sheikh Wassim and later others who wanted to generate a lifestyle and a following for themselves. I no longer had access to resources besides my Deen and my husband. For my spiritual life, I had to go within. It felt like a wilderness and a completely different world to make sense of.

I gathered myself and focused on the task ahead. My Islam, my family, the children and their future. I could no longer think about my own wishes, to stay in the circles around Sheikh, or the way of the Sufi. It was time to take control of the journey, the way of all our lives. We got back into the Jeep and crossed the bridge over to Canada, where we had everything except Sheikh.

During the long drive back, I turned around and looked at the children. Adilia was four, and her sister Amina, almost two. They were strapped into their car seats again. Amina had finally fallen asleep, her head lolling to one side. Her clothes were crumpled and dirty. She had to sleep in them because I hadn't been able to do any laundry. In place of a beloved toy that had been lost on the voyage, she was clutching an old crib blanket. Her older sister, with tangled hair, gazed out of the window at the Trans-Canada and occasionally tried to kick the seat back in front of her, but her legs were too short. "Are we there yet?" she asked, looking at me with pleading eyes.

All around us were cars coming and going from family vacations, while my family had spent over a week chasing after Sheikh's caravan, waiting around mosque car parks and unfurnished rooms because the parents were hoping to get some sort of magical interaction with an up-and-coming spiritual star. All the time, I had been irritable, tired, and occasionally straight-out frustrated, feeding them here and there, their sleep schedule completely messed up, scrambling to meet their basic needs.

However, I was not a refugee. I had a choice and the possibility of having done this completely differently, but I had not exercised it. I was free, after all. *Had this "vacation" been happy and enjoyable?* I asked myself. *Was this the just way? The right way?* I felt an overwhelming sense of shame at my answer: *It was not fair to them.*

Suddenly, Adilia was banging her fist on the window and rocking excitedly, "Oscar Meyer! Oscar Meyer!"

Over the highway median was a wiener-and-bun-shaped car, the Oscar Meyer custom-made car, making its way across Canada over the summer. This was our time to see it! Serendipity! So, we all burst into the publicity song, "Oh, I wish I were an Oscar Meyer Weiner . . . !" for a while and that lifts our exhausted spirits and makes us laugh. When I see the roller coaster of Canada's Wonderland in the distance, I have an affirmative, positive idea . . . the first in a while. "Let's stop and go in!" and we do.

The photo of us as a family with Sheikh resurfaced, synchronously, with the writing of this memoir. It helped me to piece together what had happened, how it was that the all-encompassing presence of Sheikh Nazim in my life had been lost, like incense smoke through an open window. As I was preparing this memoir for publication, it vanished, evaporating again. I looked everywhere but it would not be found. *Is there significance in this?* I asked myself. *Of course there is, and on the level that I see it, the absence is completely right. When we parted from Sheikh at Niagara Falls, I had also unconsciously left the tariquat.*

The central place of the Sheikh had gone, although there were still echoes in the crashing of the river falling over the rocks, the river you never stand in twice.

❖   ❖   ❖

I had surrendered my will, mind and heart to the tariquat. I told myself their structure could guide me and my family. I imagined that Sheikh Nazim's spiritual worldview would be the best one for me and my family. There had already been suggestions that Ibrahim give up psychiatry and move to the Middle East, and then this course of action had been demanded. Ibrahim really wanted to escape his psychiatric practice and the turbulence at the Sufi centre. He consulted Sheikh Nazim on this and other issues and had received the directive. The last life-altering decision, made without my input, was that the family should leave Canada to move to Cairo, Egypt, one of the most polluted cities in the world.

"If not Egypt, then Jordan! Why she is always refusing?" was the message from Sheikh Nazim conveyed to me by Ibrahim. I was not able to act otherwise and did not have other alternatives.

I remembered how it felt when, just after giving birth to my third daughter, I had to pack up the home in Ville St. Laurent, which had been sold by the owner, not us. I remembered how I feared another immigration, another "new country," once again a stranger immersed in another culture and language I didn't understand. I remembered how my new baby Sara didn't gain weight at first because I had no milk, how a Chinese doctor advised me to drink broth before and after each feed.

A new Muslim convert came to help and support me in the dark days before we had left Montreal, while I wept and tried to nurse my new baby during the post-natal depression. There was nothing from the many Naqshbandi we had hosted and helped over the years. I told myself that they were just doing what they were told or just going with the sort of "groupthink" that pulled their strings. When I arrived in London, on the way to Egypt, I felt the betrayal on many levels, but it also became clear to me the injustices that so many others had suffered after we spoke with some of the mureeds there who had simply left under the new order.

I remember being at Mirabel airport with our suitcases stuffed and strapped shut. They were too heavy. I had packed all the children's winter coats and clothes as well as my own. We had no room for toys or baby equipment. I had to take out as much as I could to make the bags lighter, but I couldn't. They needed their coats and their hats. I had already pared down our possessions to the minimum. "Ya Allah, Ya Latif," I said as I sank to the floor, weeping.

My mind began disintegrating, and I felt like I was falling down a well and I could see the walls rippling as I passed down and down and I couldn't stop, I couldn't stop crying. I cried for weeks back in London, once more at my mother's flat. In England, I refused to be hospitalized or go on medication because I did not want to compromise the baby. Staying with my mother, I was able to rest while Ibrahim went on ahead to Cairo to find an apartment and work. The more I distanced myself from the Naqshbandi, the better I felt.

The children went to school in Mill Hill, and the baby gained weight and smiled. Gradually, the tears stopped, and the genuine healing began months later when I attended a Mawlid with a group who allowed me to be who I was—a Western convert to Islam with a Sufi heart. Allah, in his infinite generosity, sent me a new spiritual connection. The Ba Alawi Habaib—and, specifically, Sheikh Abu Bakr Abdullah and his lovely wife, Khadijah—restored my faith, sanity, and hope. They provided me with a new way, a pure path, and I remained a Muslim. My faith survived, unlike that of other converts.

From that, I learned the most important lesson of the Sufi Path.

You will be alone on Judgment Day, and you will face your Lord. You will answer for all your actions and decisions, good and bad. Why would you let anyone get in the way of your relationship with the true centre of your being, with the source of the creation of the world and everything in it, with Allah? Always remember your Imam, your heart, your life, and your reward now and in the afterlife.

I realized it wasn't Allah, or the Quran, or the Prophet Muhammad (PBUH), who was saying I should go to Egypt, who was saying that I should produce male children, who was saying I should simply do what I was told even when it felt wrong. I realized that I did not need a Sheikh to tell me how to live. I had put a fallible human being in control of my life, and that was an error. There was nothing else to believe and trust in, other than Allah.

It's become clear to me we are made by Allah's love and compassion and that we are given the unbelievable blessing of a human life. We are given the opportunity to do the best our hearts can in any time and any situation. We are here by the will of Allah.

By the will of Allah, Ibrahim caught hepatitis in Egypt and became seriously sick. When he had recovered enough to travel, we then went back to Montreal. After lots of duahs, the following year, we were back in Montreal at Bubby's house in Dollard des Ormeaux, where she and Zayde were very happy to welcome us. Ibrahim's family helped us to buy our own home and reestablish our family.

'Inshallah' or 'Not Tonight'.

❧

S everal years later, at our comfortable home in the West Island of Montreal, the phone rang around suppertime on a weeknight, and even though I usually wouldn't answer it, an inner compulsion made me pick up.

A heavily accented male voice was speaking. "Hello, Salaams. I am calling to tell you that Maulana Sheikh Nazim will be visiting Montreal, and you are invited to a reception in his honour at my house."

Well, that was nice. I felt sure that if Wassim was issuing the invitations, I certainly wouldn't have got one. I didn't know who this man was, he must have got the phone number from a mutual friend. I briefly considered going, then I excused myself, saying that it was a weeknight and that I would "pass the message on to my husband" although he was away at a medical conference.

The man on the call was insistent, perhaps "acting under orders." He would not displease the Sheikh in this honour of hospitality.

"Inshallah, I will come," a very non-committal reply, frequently used to say "no," but without conveying the offensive sense of refusing the invitation, implying somehow that it is part of the divine decree whether you will be there, and, in addition, implying a holiness and submission which you really don't have. Although if a miraculous chain of events were to provide me with a babysitter and a ride there and back "Cinderella-style," then yeah, I might have gone.

Over the next few days, I remembered with a warm heart all the kindness I had received from Sheikh and especially his family in Cyprus. I remembered the camaraderie and fellowship among the mureeds at one time. I reflected on how I had tried so hard to live like an Ottoman and then remembered what a relief it had been when I had dropped the burden. I just settled for being an ordinary Muslim, living an ordinary life—albeit with some extraordinary friends. I didn't have the stamina for more adventures.

Another evening later in the week, the phone rang. I didn't answer, and when the answering machine clicked on, they hung up. The phone rang again; I didn't answer. Then the phone rang again. Perhaps there was an accident or an emergency and I was just being an idiot and avoiding important vital calls from the rest of the world?

I picked it up. There was a lot of noise in the background, a crowd of people talking. It sounded like a party or a wedding reception. Over the hubbub, this time a different male voice was shouting so he could be heard above the din.

"The Maulana Sheikh is asking for the Munirah. He is asking where she is ..."

This, unfortunately, I admit, was not the first time I had not been in Sheikh's company when expected. There were times in Peckham when I had also been absent from his lectures and other times in Cyprus when I had just left.

"Oh," I said. "Please send my apologies. I cannot come."

"Why? Why? You must come! The Sheikh is asking!"

"No," I heard myself saying firmly.

Suddenly, I am wanted there at this reception in an undoubtingly huge house? Why? I wondered silently. Why now? I wasn't wanted or needed when I was trailing around after your entourage a few summers back. I wasn't wanted or needed when you told my husband to go live in Egypt and take us all with him. No, I wasn't even consulted, and now I am wanted? What had changed? Well, I had changed and my priorities also. Whatever this was, it was not part of my to-do list.

In a spiteful twist, referencing for effect my Muslim submission to the patriarchy but fudging the reality that I could come and go as I wanted, I said, "I don't have my husband's permission to leave the house, and he isn't here. I must take care of my children, and they have to be up early to go to school tomorrow so, no thanks." I had also decided that I was not going to put them, or myself, through any more experiences around Sheikh or his mureeds.

Whoever he was did not speak for a while. I thought I heard a gasp, but perhaps it was something else. I couldn't be sure because of all the background noise, people with their demands, their adoration, their gifts to Sheikh in exchange for duahs and favours. The call ended abruptly with Salaams.

❖   ❖   ❖

I'm still not sure if it was a "break up" with Sheikh Nazim or if it was a "broke off" from the Naqshbandis. Either way, something definitively snapped at the Falls and was damaged further in the aftermath, the difficult birth of my third child and the order to move from Canada. My heart and my healing meant then that I had to distance myself from it all and what it had become as much as possible. That remains the case today.

Sometimes, when a relationship ends, it's the small stuff, the little things. There were always issues right there in the beginning, but for love, you chose to overlook them. Eventually, you reach a boiling point, and then something blows the lid off. The force to stay in the relationship is not equal to the freedom and possibility of going, and so, you leave.

There may also be a natural, normal course of events. A seed produces a shoot, which is nourished in the right conditions and grows into a fine tree, which produces fruit and is abundant and blessed. There are many metaphors in the Quran about a good tree. Trees are also an important image in our understanding of paradise. However, trees grow old and wither. Sometimes they are cut down, and sometimes they get sick. Tariquats are like that also. Betrayal, criticism, different agendas, blame, feelings of inadequacy, and frustration all have their place on the Sufi path, just like everything else, in the natural order.

What kind of tree was the relationship with Sheikh Nazim? Once, it was a fruit tree, a plum tree with branches so heavy they fell to the ground with the weight. Then the branches split, and the sap spilled down the trunk, and insects got into the kernel of the tree. When the insects got in, we started to feel that our friend and guide just didn't see us anymore. He was looking over our shoulders at something or someone else. The season had passed. The tree was never as strong after that. There was fruit, but it had had its season of glory, and now it was older and tired. Perhaps that was just what it was.

I will tell you, though, that it should not, could not be any other way and that I would not, could not, want it to be.

The Next Generation

꙼

Decades on, and it's right there on YouTube. One of the hundreds of uploads under the search "Naqshbandi" and it goes like this.

A heavy middle-aged man with a long grey beard and a turban is leading a group of anomalous "hipster types in turbans" around a series of cemeteries and cement mosques in what looks to be communist bloc countryside. At one point, this leader is sitting on a raised wooden platform chatting, eating grapes, and drinking small glasses of tea convivially with his fellow travellers, the other men, that is.

On lower ground, below the merry group, some other people sit, trying to soothe small children and shifting about uncomfortably. There is no cohesion in this other group, no toastmaster. They are hunched and unhappy looking, almost awkward, not really knowing what to do with themselves, being in this position and not really being happy about it. For they are the women, and so have been given only a minor, supporting role in this, despite their drive and enthusiasm. The men continue for quite a few minutes in this short film, sharing their brotherhood and their bonding time. They enjoy this "hanging out."

Are they really oblivious to the discomfort of their wives and children? Have they accepted a narrative where women are always complaining, and it is tiresome and ungodly?

I gasped in astonishment. This video was made a few years ago, but it was all the same as it had been when I'd left decades before. Different faces under the turbans, different languages and locations, but these images illustrate the same old story.

So here is another version. A fairy story that fulfills a fantasy of alternative outcomes. This time, one of those women, a known troublemaker, notorious for her bad temper and mischief-making, stands up and starts to speak.

Her authority drowns out "the boys," and they put down their beads and tooth sticks and listen, shocked and surprised. This isn't how it is supposed to be. This hasn't been authorized by the Sheikh, although it may have been predicted.

* * *

A while later, Ibrahim and I are happily divorced, but he invites me to go to a café near the Plateau Montreal to meet our old friend Abdul Hamid. Curiosity and nostalgia combine because my life is very different from what it was when I was in the Naqshbandi tariquat. The new version, rebranded as "Haqqani," has exploded worldwide and is very present on social media. I don't know how many followers there are now, and I don't have any contact with them. I have "moved on," as they say, and have discovered other spiritual resources which have sustained and nurtured my faith.

The café is owned by a lovely Tuareg man and it is mid-week, mid-morning. It's almost empty. He lets us wait while next door, in the Naqshbandi centre, Sheikh Abdul Hamid is giving advice and making duah for those who have shown up, pleading for help in any form.

Eventually, about twelve male mureeds troop in and seat themselves in a row along a cushioned bench near the floor. They are almost identical, but there are individual variations. Some wear floor-length green coats, some long waistcoats and baggy shirts. All wear variations of the Syrian/Turkish sherwal pants. They all wear the standard green pointed hat with turban fabric wrapped around it, some white, some in other colours. This may be the result of Sheikh Nazim's whimsical idea that his mureeds should wear the colours of different "nations," regardless of their country of origin.

They sit and stare and mumble their tesbih while we wait for Abdul Hamid to make his entrance. I think of starlings on a wire waiting for the signal to migrate or, in a more secular context, a government office, although nobody has a number. Although I am right in front of them, they do not make any eye contact or acknowledge my presence.

"Salaam alaikum, Munirah."

Abdul Hamid greets me warmly, and it is a relief to see someone who is coming from an actual place of heart and humanity and not a role. Through the years, he has remained true to his vocation and the Sufi path. Although he must have ignored the worst of the Haqqani actions, he has managed to stay in touch with his heart and his practices.

"Wa alaikum as salaam," I reply.

Abdul Hamid settles down in the middle of the line, and there is an awkward pause while I glare at the starlings, and they glare back. We are united in our misunderstanding of what the other is doing. Perhaps I am giving off the wrong signals in my clothing and attitude. I'm wearing Western "office casual," although I have a headscarf draped loosely over my hair. I am sitting at a table with my legs crossed.

I ask, thinking of the owner and his need to run a business, if anyone would like a coffee. Then I recognized one of them, although I hadn't at first. We go back a long way. I don't have good memories. Nobody says anything, and I have already had coffee, I don't want another.

"No need." Abdul Hamid raises his hand, and it is a gesture directly from Sheikh Nazim. It is astonishing. It is as if Sheikh Nazim has become inculcated in him. I'm comforted, though, that the real Sheikh Nazim is still present in this way. In any way, that is the prism of truth that I knew.

As the "starling chat" continues, I start to feel triggered, and anger rises in me. Of course, as a woman, they all completely ignore me. In their opinion, I have no right to be there. These men sitting around in their costumes like actors at a film shoot between takes strikes me as both pretentious and ridiculous in any context. Despite the narrative that they are "polishing their hearts," I'm not feeling the love of any polished hearts reflecting the light of Allah. Only Abdul Hamid seems to have any humility and presence, and that has been earned over many, many years. I can't imagine how he has stuck it out for so long.

I don't have a turban, but it is my turn to speak. I interrupt the chat because I feel compelled to tell them a story. This is what, as an educator, we refer to as "a teaching moment." I want to shake them up and tell them a simple reality, a small part of what I learned, hanging around the movement.

"Once, I asked Sheikh Nazim, 'What is the best way for me to make spiritual progress'?'"

I remember a polished wooden dining table in Famagusta at the house of a family connected to Sheikh by marriage. I was on one side, and he was on the other. My question was pressing and urgent. It has been a few weeks since I entered the tariquat and I was still waiting for subtle esoteric teachings that would enlighten and transform me.

"At that time, I thought that you entered the tariquat and then poof, like magic, you became enlightened and entered a very high spiritual station. That there was some technique, or meditation system, or duah that would magically transform me into a Sufi."

I had really thought it was that simple. I had become Muslim, taken bayaat, got married, was wearing hijab, all the outward stuff. The "lady of the house" had tried to answer my question instead of the Sheikh. She probably wanted to instruct me on domestic duties and manners, but fortunately, someone interrupted her and insisted that Sheikh answer.

Sheikh Nazim narrowed his eyes slightly as he paused to consider. The room was silent except for the sound of his beads clicking. He closed his eyes briefly and then spoke.

"Sheikh said, 'You know the difference between the right way and the wrong way. Now you must choose the right way.'"

This hadn't seemed like enough information. I struggled to understand what he was referring to.

"You believe in Almighty Allah, the One God?"

"Yes."

"You believe in his Messengers?"

"Yes."

"The Angels, the Djinn and the Day of Judgment?"

"Yes."

"You believe in the Books and Revelation?"

"Yes."

"You believe in the Judgment and the Day of Resurrection?"

That one was a bit scary to think about, but I said yes.

"Then you must make your Salat five times a day, and you must support and maintain the five pillars of Islam. Fasting, Zakat, and the Hajj, when you are able."

"At the time, I was a bit shocked by this interaction. I had hoped for some deep "Ninja"-style initiation but over the years, thirty years later, I see the wisdom of this method. If we practice Islam with sincerity and dedication and we have our connection through Bayat with our Sheikh and the Silsila, we have all we really need to sustain us spiritually for much of our life."

My story was finished. Abdul Hamid smiled warmly and nodded. I had tried to give the new mureeds an "Aha! moment," but it was way out of line. They stared straight ahead in silence, bored, irritated or something else. Who am I to tell them about their tariquat!? I do not have a franchise certificate from the inner circle. I have not been working in the kitchen, providing meals for them. The tension hangs in the air as my anecdotal wisdom is discarded. I have no credibility in their eyes. My insight, intuition, and path are irrelevant in this context. Then, more awkward silence until the old associate leans forward and says, "I'll take a coffee."

He knows that I am paying.

Flying over Cyprus

❧

In the summer of 2007, I was on a plane heading to Damascus, Syria. Blessed and fortunate to be living the dream of teaching English for the summer at the British Council. I had temporarily left our home and the girls, now teen-agers, in the care of Ibrahim. I was driven by a passion to reconnect with what was essential to me. In a way, it was also to extend a hand to a former self and find again my reason to be.

Sliding up the plastic window cover, I saw a rising golden dawn reflected in the smooth Mediterranean Sea. To my surprise, right there was the familiar lute shape and Cyprus below. No buildings or lights were visible, but in the morning light, I could see a tawny ridge of mountains and some smooth plains of green and beige.

As the plane curved, I traced the shoreline of the right coast at the north end, the handle. I tried to see Nicosia, Famagusta, and maybe Lefkonica.

I knew he was there. I'd seen many photographs on social media of him as he was at that time, toward the end of his life. They were shared among his millions of followers. It was not the Sheikh Nazim I knew or remembered. He had sunk into a large armchair. It was hard for him to move around. He couldn't travel. His hooded, beautiful eyes gazed far away from his confinement.

"As salaam alaikum, Munirah," a voice in my head said clearly.

"Wa lakum as salaam," I replied reflexively before my astonishment took hold.

I tried to make sense of this and then just dismissed my confusion and moved into this other state of consciousness. There was no more time to waste, no more distractions.

Deep emotion welled up as I was once more in his presence. He was there, and so was I, suspended in some kind of space continuum. It had been decades, but time and distance had folded into a wrinkle.

"Thank you," I said after a pause when I felt the sadness, regret, and love arise. I witnessed them, and tears came into my eyes. The veils of the heart were dissolved, and underneath was joy.

"Thank you for all you did and for everything that came to pass."

He nodded silently. I could see him. We rested in a convivial place of peace and friendship. I understood that he was the servant of Allah, and so was I, in my own way. On the terms I needed for my own understanding.

Nothing more was said, and there were no more thoughts or reactions. I became intensely conscious of his presence next to me, almost as close as the jugular vein. Then, from the rising sun, golden light burst all around. The cabin was filled with it. I became aware that this extraordinary light extended far outside the cabin, outside of time and space and distance. There was no me. There was no Sheikh. Only a radiant light that reached further than the heavens and deeper than the sea and the tawny earth.

This light went with me, on to Damascus, to the Mosque of Ibn Arabi, to the hill of Mount Qasyun, where Grand Sheikh Abdullah is buried.

Glossary

A

- adab: Courtesy and manners.
- awrad: An individual recitation for dhikr done on an individual daily basis.
- awliya: Friends (of Allah) (plural of "wali").
- ayats: Verses of the Quran.
- azan: Call to prayer.

B

- barakat: Spiritual blessing
- bayaat: An oath of allegiance to a Sufi teacher.
- bida: What is considered by some scholars to be an Islamic innovation in religion.
- Bismillah (hir rahman nir raheem): A phrase recited before an activity in order to remember Allah, literally, "In the name of Allah, the most beneficent, the most merciful."

D

- dawah: Introducing the teachings of Islam to non-Muslims or lapsed Muslims.
- dars: lesson or exposition from a religious text
- dhikr: Remembrance (of Allah).
- duah: Individual prayers in Arabic.
- deen: Way of life, religion, path of righteousness to Allah.

E

- estafrullah (transliterated Turkish) for "I seek forgiveness from Allah": A petition for redemption.

F

- Fajr: Muslim dawn prayer.
- fana fi Allah (Arabic): The ultimate spiritual goal of merging the individual with divine reality
- fana fi Sheikh: A station in Sufism where the individual is merged with the divine reality that the Sheikh is carrying.
- fard: Religious duties and obligations.
- Fatihah: The first chapter of the Quran, which is translated as "The Opening."
- fatwa: Religious ruling or opinion from qualified source.
- fitnah: Strife, sedition of authority, civil unrest.

H

- hal: a spiritual station or state of consciousness
- Hajja: title given to a female Muslim who has made the pilgrimage to Mecca
- Hanafi: one of the 4 schools of Islamic jurisprudence. Founded by Imam Abu Hanifa
- haram: unlawful in religious law
- hijab: Head covering worn by a Muslim woman.

I

- iftar: "Breaking the fast," a Ramadan social occasion.
- Imam: A religious leader who leads prayers at the mosque.
- Iman: A believer's recognition of faith and deeds, e.g., the six articles of faith.
- Istikhara: The prayer for guidance.

J

- Jihad al-nafs: the personal struggle to fight against evil, anger and other negative human qualities.

- juz: one of the thirty equal parts of the Quran.

K

- Kaaba: a cloth covered stone cube shaped building at the centre of Mecca built by Prophet Ibrahim
- kufr: To conceal or disbelieve in Allah, also used to refer to disbelief in the teachings of Islam.

L

- Lailat al Qadr: Blessed night during the month of Ramadan.

M

- madh'hab ("mezheb" Turk): A school of thought within Islamic jurisprudence
- mashallah: Literally, "God has willed it," commonly used to express appreciation, thankfulness, and awe.
- miswaq: teeth-cleaning stick, a sunnah of Prophet Muhammed (PBUH).
- mosque: House of prayer in Islam, aka Masjid.
- mureed: A disciple of a Sufi master who has taken an oath of allegiance (bayaat).

N

- nafs: Lower, wilful self.
- Nour: Spiritual Light specifically an attribute (name) of Allah

P

- PBUH: Peace and blessings be upon him.
- purdah: the seclusion of women from men they are not related to.

Q

- qibla: The direction Muslims face when praying toward the Kaaba in Mecca, Saudi Arabia

S

Salat: Prayer, the five daily.

- Salat al Asr: Afternoon prayer.
- Salat al Dhuhr: Noon prayer.
- Salat al Fajr: Dawn prayer.
- Salat al Jummah: Friday prayer.
- Salat al Maghrib: Sunset prayer.
- Shafi'i (madh'hab): school of law and religious interpretation developed by Imam al Shafi'i
- Shahada: Testimony of faith in Islam.
- Shaitain: Devil.
- sheikh: A Sufi spiritual guide, a teacher.
- shirk: Associating partners with Allah, it is considered a major sin in Islam.
- silsala: "Chain, link, connection" lineage and spiritual genealogy.
- Sirat al-Mustiqueem: "The straight path." In Islam, the path to God.
- satsang (Hindu): sitting in the company of blessed teachers to gain access to higher levels of consciousness
- sunnah: The way of life and practices of the Prophet Muhammad (PBUH).

T

- Tahajuud: "Keeping vigil." A night prayer reciting Quran and praying.
- tajweed: method of correctly reciting the Qu'ran using stops and pauses as transmitted.
- Taraweeh: A voluntary prayer performed by Muslims during Ramadan.
- tariquat: A mystical brotherhood of Sufis who focus on spirituality.
- tekke: Turkish word for Sufi lodge, hospice, or residence.
- tesbih: A set of prayer beads to engage in remembrance.

U

- Ummah: The community of Muslims throughout the world.

W

- Wahhabi(ism): A conservative branch of Sunni Islam.
- wakeel: An agent or deputy who acts on behalf of another person, in marriage on behalf of the bride.

- wali: Friend (of Allah).
- waswas: Whispers from Shaitan.
- Wird: A daily practice involving specific ayah, prayers and supplications.
- wudu: Ablutions for purification before the prayer.

Z

- Zakat: Charity.
- zawiya: A Sufi centre.
- zikr: See *dhikr*.